Other Books by Chet Cataldo:

Spiritual Portrait of A Believer

Ancient Aliens, The Rapture and the Return of Christ

When Your Name is Called:
A Study on the Day of Judgment

A Life Beyond

CHOSEN:
A STUDY IN THE DOCTRINE OF ELECTION

CHET CATALDO

authorHOUSE®

AuthorHouse™
1663 Liberty Drive
Bloomington, IN 47403
www.authorhouse.com
Phone: 1-800-839-8640

Published by AuthorHouse   11/11/2013

ISBN: 978-1-4918-3103-8 (sc)
ISBN: 978-1-4918-3104-5 (e)

Library of Congress Control Number: 2013919542

To the Saints through the ages who have
stood for Scriptural Christianity in the face of
opposition, fears and doubts.

CONTENTS

Introduction.. ix

Chapter 1   Election is primarily corporate.................. 1

Chapter 2   Human Responsibility and
             Apostasy in relation to Election................21

Chapter 3   God's decrees are not fixed (closed) 76

Chapter 4   Hardening of the heart............................. 92

Chapter 5   Chosen in Christ..................................... 111

Chapter 6   Free Will and Free Grace........................ 131

INTRODUCTION

The doctrine of election has split the Christian Church over its interpretation. This doctrine is understood in two different ways. The first understanding is that God has decided, chosen beforehand, in ages past, both what will happen to people and who will spend eternity in heaven. In other words, this camp teaches that God chooses certain individuals who will go to heaven and leaves all the rest to go to hell.

The second understanding holds the view that election, chosen is a description of those who choose to believe in and commit their lives to Jesus Christ as Lord and Savior. This view states that within the plans, decrees of God is room for human response, faith and even rejection. God does not, according to the second understanding, decide beforehand what will happen to people and who will go to heaven and hell.

The doctrine of election, not only has split the Church but has also caused the hearts of many sincere Christians to tremble, fear and at times even give up. The present study is an attempt to explain the Biblical teaching on the doctrine of election. The doctrine of election is a teaching that is found within the total teaching of Scripture. Because the meaning of election is found within the total teaching of Scripture; this study will examine both the teaching of the Old Testament and the teaching of the New Testament in an attempt to understand the meaning of election. In addition, because Paul mentions election in the epistle to the Romans, it is important to place the doctrine of election within the total theological teaching of the Gospel. The reason for doing this is both Jesus' and Paul's statements. Paul stated that the Gospel he received, he received by a revelation of Jesus Christ (Galatians 1: 11-12). The statement of Jesus is that He came to fulfill the Old Testament (Matthew 5:17). Thus, the meaning of election is to be found within the total theological understanding of the Gospel itself.

In the attempt to understand the total Biblical teaching on election, the following topics will be examined: Election as primarily corporate and not the choosing of certain individuals; how human responsibility relates to apostasy; God's decrees, whether they are fixed from all eternity or is there room within the decrees of God for human choice; the hardening of the heart, in this discussion, the heart of Pharaoh will be examined; what it means to be chosen *in* Christ and finally does free will truly exist and how the will of human beings relates to free grace.

It is my prayer that this study will contribute to the Church's understanding of election and at the same time will ease the hearts of many of my Christian sisters and brothers.

CHAPTER 1

ELECTION IS PRIMARILY CORPORATE

The teaching of election/predestination is causing a great divide in the Church of Jesus Christ. In addition to this divide, this teaching is also causing much anguish of soul for countless individual Christians. Many base their view of election/predestination on Romans 9. It is vital to understand what Paul was saying in both Romans 9 and the context of the whole letter to the Romans in order to understand the Scriptural message regarding election/predestination.

To understand the message of Paul in Romans, we must read/understand what Paul wrote from a Jewish perspective. So, we begin with reading Romans 1-9 read from a Jewish perspective. The mindset, the belief of the Jewish people is that God was God of Israel and you, the Jewish race, were his people (Deuteronomy 7:6). In addition, you believed that God would never leave you (Deuteronomy 31:8). Then when you read Romans 1-8, you read what was totally antithetical to what you had been taught. What you read was Paul writing that the Gospel is now for everyone (Romans 1:16). When you read that, everything within you cried out in disagreement. You cried that the Jews alone were the special people of God.

1

Reading further in Romans you read that the Jews were storing up wrath against yourself as a people and you as an individual in day of wrath (Romans 2:2-5). A further teaching of Romans 1-9 is that the Gentiles are now seen equally as people of circumcision (2:25-29). Circumcision, you were taught was the mark of belonging to God. Now, Paul is saying that it matters not whether a person is circumcised or not. As you were trying to understand what Paul said about circumcision, there is the further shock of the rejection of the Jews and the inclusion of the Gentiles. This went against everything that you have been taught; everything that you lived; everything that you are. As your whole being was convulsing, you then read that the Law was insufficient because righteousness is apart from the Law (Romans 3:21) and apart from circumcision (4:9-12). In fact, the law, instead of being the answer, caused sin to increase (Romans 5:20); stimulated sin (Romans 7:9) and was the cause of death (Romans 7:13).

The natural question a Jew, even a convert to Christianity from the Jewish people would ask Paul is: did he, Paul, ignore the Old Testament in his understanding and preaching of the Gospel?

These are the issues Paul addresses in Romans 9-11.[1] When Romans is read, we come to the conclusion that

---

[1]   G. Osborne, *Romans*, (Downers Grove: InterVarsity Press, 2004), 233.

Paul was aware of the Jewish reaction to the Gospel. In Romans 3:1-4, Paul was addressing the some of the advantages of being a Jew. He continues discussing the advantages of being a Jew in Romans 9: 4, 5. However, here, Paul is addressing the objection that some within the Jewish community and some of those who believed in Christ from the Jewish community had that there is no advantage of being from the Jewish community. Paul answers that objection by stating that there are advantages of being from the Jewish community.

Paul goes on to address another of the objections that arose from the Jewish community. Based on what Paul wrote, the Jewish understanding is that if what Paul is saying regarding the Jews, Gentiles and the Law, then God would be unfaithful. Paul's answer to this objection is that God is faithful even in the midst of Jewish unfaithfulness (Romans 3: 5-6).

A third objection that arose is that if what Paul wrote was true, then the Law was nullified (Romans 3: 31). Paul answers this objection in his discussion regarding Abraham and the basis for Abraham's acceptance with God (Romans 4). Paul, going back to the Old Testament, reminds the objectors that Abraham was accepted by God based on his faith in God (Romans 4:3). Paul, then states that the teaching that acceptance with God is based on faith and not the Law is a consistent teaching throughout the Old Testament. To do this Paul quoted David in Psalm 32: 1, 2. Paul understood David as saying that righteousness is apart from works, apart from the Law (Romans 4:6-8).

Paul, after showing from the Old Testament that righteousness is by faith and apart from the Law, then asks: is this righteousness for the circumcised only, that is for the Jews or is righteousness by faith also for the uncircumcised, that is for Gentiles as well (Romans 4:9)? Paul, in asking this question is answering also the objection that circumcision, according to Paul, was nullified, made void and the objection that the Gentiles could not be included within the people of God because the Jews were the special people of God.

To answer these objections, Paul asked if righteousness by faith and apart from the Law is for the circumcised only or were the Gentiles also included? To answer this, Paul once again refers to Abraham and states that Abraham was reckoned, was considered righteous when he was uncircumcised (Romans 4:10). Abraham, while uncircumcised, believed God and God considered Abraham righteous. After being reckoned as righteous, Abraham received circumcision (Romans 4: 11). Circumcision then was a sign of faith righteousness.

It is important, at this point for us to understand the relationship that God established with Abraham. God called Abraham and said to him that God would make Abraham a great nation and through Abraham that the whole world would be blessed (Genesis 12: 1-3). Paul states that Abraham was both an individual and the father of the faith (Romans 4:11, 12). He goes on to say that the promise given by God to Abraham and his seed that they would be heir of the world was not through the law (Romans 4:13) but it was through faith (Romans 4:16).

Paul then takes his understanding of Abraham and faith to include both the circumcised who believed and the uncircumcised who believe (Romans 4:16). By this understanding we are to conclude that the relationship between God and His people was a faith relationship. This is understood from the fact that circumcision was both a sign of Abraham's righteousness by faith and circumcision was also a sign of the covenant that God established with Abraham and his seed (Genesis 17:11). From this understanding, Paul is stating that God's relationship from the beginning of His covenant with His people was a faith relationship.

Paul clarifies the object of faith righteousness. He states that the object of faith righteous is not the law but is Jesus our Lord (Romans 4:23-25) who died for sins and was raised to life for justification[2] (Romans 4: 24, 25).

A further objection that arose from Paul's explanation of the Gospel can be called antinomianism. Antinomianism means against the law. What this objection states is that if the law is not the basis for a right relationship with God, then there are no moral restraints and that people can do whatever they want (Romans 6:1). Paul's answer is that faith righteousness is both death to sin and life to God in Christ (Romans 6: 2-14). When a person believes in Christ, that person dies and is given a new life. This new life is a life that has been freed from sin (Romans 6:6, 7). Paul goes on to state that this new life is a life offered to God (Romans 6:13) for the purpose of living out righteousness (Romans 6:13). Paul goes on to explain that this new life in Christ is a life lived of whole hearted, willing obedience (Romans 6:17) and is a life where the Christian is a willing slave to righteousness (Romans 6:18). To be a slave to righteousness means that we are right with God and we desire to live ethically according to God's standards.[3] Paul is not teaching sinless perfection

---

[2]   The Greek word is dikaiosis which means to cause someone to be in a right relation with someone else by setting them free from their sin (J. Louw & E. Nida, *Greek-English Lexicon of the New Testament based on Sematic Domains,* New York: United Bible Societies, 1989, 557).

[3]   Osborne, *Romans,* 163.

here. This is understood when he writes that we are to reckon, consider ourselves dead to sin (Romans 6:11) and that we are to not let sin reign over us (Romans 6:12).

Because Paul states that righteousness is by faith apart from the law, there arose the thought that the law was not only worthless but was sin (Romans7:7). Paul answers this by stating that the purpose of the law was to reveal sin (Romans 7:7, 13). He further states that the law is both holy (Romans 7:12) and spiritual (Romans 7:14). Paul states that the Law had its purpose. However, when Christ came, although the law was completer in him, the law in Christ was fulfilled (Matthew 5:17); so both the law and the rituals were no longer essential.[4]

Paul, coming out of his presentation of the Gospel and the previous objections that arose from Christians who came out of the Jewish community and perhaps some still in the Jewish community, clarifies in Romans 9-11a further truth concerning God, Israel and the means of salvation. The truth that Paul clarifies in Romans 9-11 is the fact that God is sovereign and can choose the means of salvation.

In the previous chapters of Romans, Paul demonstrated that righteousness, salvation, a right relationship with God is by faith apart from the Law. Paul has shown by his use

---

[4]   *Ibid*, 233.

of the Old Testament that faith has been God's method of making right human beings from the very beginning.

The fact of the many objections to the Gospel that arose, points to the fact that the Jewish community understood very differently than what Paul made clear through his presentation of the Gospel.

Paul in Romans 9-11 shows even more clearly that the popular Jewish understanding of Israel and her relationship with God is an incorrect understanding. He does this by pointing out what constitutes true Israel (Romans 9:6). By the phrase *true Israel* Paul means the people of God. Thus, we are to understand that in Romans 9-11 Paul's primary purpose is to make clear what constitutes the people of God.

Paul begins Romans 9 with his deep heart felt desire that his country men, that is the Jewish community, would believe in Christ and experience salvation, that is true righteousness (Romans 9:1-5). While that is Paul's deep heart desire, he returns to his main point in this section which is to make clear who constitutes the people of God.

He starts out by stating that within the physical people of Israel are two groups. If we used Paul's terms we would state that these two groups are: Israel and non-Israel (Romans 9:6). The collective/group of people who are *non-Israel* are physically descended from Abraham (Romans 9:7); yet, these are not the children of Abraham, or to use another phrase; they are not Abraham's seed (Romans 9:7). Paul is able to make this distinction because God had said to Abraham that it was through Isaac that his offspring, his seed, his children would be counted (Romans 9: 7). God said to Abraham that it was through Isaac that his offspring would come because Abraham had two sons at the time. One son, Ishmael, was the child of Abraham and Hagar. The second son, Isaac was the child of Abraham and Sarah. God had said to Abraham and to Sarah that it was through their union that a son would be born, the child of promise (Romans 9:9). We see in this that although Isaac and Ishmael having different mothers shared the same father, Abraham. Because God had promised to Abraham and to his children that they were to constitute the people of God; Abraham was informed by God that it was through Isaac, the child of promise that his children would come and not through his son Ishmael (Romans 9:8). What we are to understand is that just because there are people who are descendants of Abraham does not mean that they are children of Abraham. The discussion is over natural children versus children of the promise (9:8), children of faith and not through the flesh. Within, Israel, then are two groups, the children of Isaac and the children of Ishmael. The children of Isaac were the children of the promise while the children of Ishmael were the children of the flesh.

Paul, further narrowing down the people which constitute the people of God, states that even amongst the children of Isaac, the people of God are to be seen as a very narrow group of the whole (Romans 9:10). While Isaac and Ishmael had different mothers, the children of Isaac had the same mother (Romans 9:10). A further distinction between Isaac and Ishmael was that the children of Isaac were the children of the promise; the children of Ishmael were the children of the flesh. In the sons of Isaac, both sons were of the *promised line*.[5] Yet, one was to be the children of God and the other was not.

It is vital to understand that while Jacob and Esau were individuals, they were also nations (Genesis 25:23). We are told that when Rebekah had conceived, she carried twins within her womb. When the babies jostled with each other, Rebekah inquired of the Lord and asked why this was happening (Genesis 25:22). As Rebekah inquired of the Lord, God said to her that two nations are in your womb (Genesis 25:23). This is seen also in Malachi 1: 2, 3 where Esau's mountains have been turned into a wasteland. This is further elaborated on in Jeremiah 49:7-11. In Jeremiah the Lord says that he will strip Esau bare; he will uncover his hiding places; his children, relatives and neighbors will perish.

---

5   *Ibid*, 244.

The use in Scripture for an individual to represent a collective is seen also in Adam who represents the human race (Romans 5:12-14). Paul writes that sin entered the world[6] through one man (Romans 5:12). This one man was Adam and the world is humanity.[7] What Paul has in mind here is the Jewish concept of corporate solidarity.[8] In other words, Adam represents all of humanity. We see the Scriptural teaching that the individual is used to represent the collective whole.

A second use of the individual to represent the whole is seen in Romans 5:15. Here Paul is contrasting/comparing Adam and Jesus. As Adam represented the whole human race in his sin; so Jesus represents the whole human race in himself and his work of grace.[9] The truth that Jesus represents the whole human race is seen in the fact that Jesus is called the Second Adam (1 Corinthians 15:45-47). The fact that Jesus is called the Second Adam does point very clearly to the fact that Jesus represents the whole human race. The line of reasoning goes as in this manner. To call Jesus the *Second Adam* he must also represent what the First Adam represented. Since the first Adam

---

[6] The Greek is kosmos which is the universe as an ordered structure and everything in it (Louw & Nida, *Greek-English Lexicon,* 1).

[7] Osborne, *Romans,* 137.

[8] *Ibid,* 137.

[9] *Ibid,* 144.

represented the whole human race; the Second Adam, Jesus must also represent the whole human race.

Jesus, as the representative of the whole human race is seen also in the teaching concerning: For whom did Christ die? This topic divides the Church of God. The answer to the question of for whom did Christ die is found in the statement that Christ came into the world to save sinners (1 Timothy 1:15). The purpose and mission of Jesus led Him into the world, cosmos, to save sinners. This word, cosmos, is used in the Bible to refer to the universe[10] and is so used in Acts 17:24 which states that God made the universe and everything in it. Cosmos at times is used for the world system and the people in it that have rejected God[11] (Galatians 6:14). The word cosmos is used to describe either the totality of God's creation, the universe or the totality of the world's system. Thus, when Paul wrote that Christ came into the world to save sinners, the meaning is either or both that Christ came into the universe or the anti-God system for the purpose of saving sinners. Jesus came to Israel, but His purpose was for the cosmos.

Paul wrote that Jesus came into the world for the purpose of saving sinners. We now ask: who are sinners?

---

[10]　J. Louw & E. Nida, *Greek-English Lexicon of the New Testament*, 1.

[11]　*Ibid*, 508.

The answer to the question: who are sinners is that sinners are the ones who sin. This leads to the question of: who are the ones who sin? Paul writes very explicitly that every single person in the world sins. He states four times in Romans 3:9-12 that every single person sins. Paul then sums up the Biblical position that all have sinned and thus are sinners (Romans 3:23).

In answering the question of for whom did Christ die? Paul brings attention to certain passages. In one of those passages, 1 Timothy 1:15, Paul says that it is a trustworthy saying and worthy of full acceptance (1 Timothy 1:15). Paul uses this phrase, *a trustworthy saying* 5 times. It is found in1 Timothy 1:15, 1Timothy 3:1; 1Timothy 4:9, 10; 2 Timothy 2:11; Titus 3:8). The phrase, *a trustworthy saying*, is used by Paul to identify an important and key teaching. What are these teachings that Paul considered key?

1 Timothy 1:15 teaches that the purpose of Christ was to save sinners who are in the cosmos.

1 Timothy 3:1 makes clear that the one who sets his heart on being a deacon desires a noble task.

1 Timothy 4:9, 10 teaches that God is the savior of all men, especially of the ones who believe.

2 Timothy 2:11 states that dying with Christ is not the end. When one dies with Christ, one also shares in His resurrection.

Titus 3:8 teaches that trust in God is seen in the doing of what is good.

When these 5 passages are looked at, what jumps to the front is that the teachings of these 5 verses are fundamental Christian teachings. The answer to the question of, for whom did Christ die, is found in a passage of Scripture that Paul claims as one of the fundamental teachings of Christianity (1 Timothy 4:9, 10). However, the statement that God is the Savior of all men is a very controversial statement.

The starting point in understanding what Paul meant in 1Timothy 4: 9, 10 is the Greek. The Greek states that God is the Savior of *all men*, panton anthropon. Panton, from pas, means the totality of any object, mass, all, every, each.[12] Anthropon from anthropos means male in certain cases but generically means human being.[13] When Paul states that God is the Savior of *everyone*, but especially of believers, he does not mean universalism, or the teaching that everyone will go to heaven. We know this because Paul writes that it is necessary to believe in Jesus Christ to be saved (Romans 10:9-13). What Paul meant when he said that God is the savior of all is that God's grace has appeared to everyone (same Greek words for *everyone* as found in 1 Timothy 4: 9, 10 are in Titus 2:11) with

---

[12]   *Ibid,* 597.

[13]   *Ibid,* 104.

the real offer of salvation (Titus 2:11). We know that the offer of salvation is a real offer, that is that Christ died for everyone because it is God's desire, the word for desire is thelo which means *to desire to have, to want*,[14] that all be saved (1 Timothy 2:4). It is also God's desire that none perish (2 Peter 3:9). The word, *perish,* which is used in 2 Peter 3:9 is also used in John 3:16 to describe what will not happen to those who believe in Jesus Christ. Because God desires all to believe and not perish, He sent His only Son to die for everyone's sin (1Timothy 2: 6). In 1Timothy 2:6 it says that Jesus gave himself as a ransom (NIV) for all. The *all* is made clear in 1 John 2:2. In 1 John 2:2 the death of Christ for everyone's sin is made abundantly clear. In this verse, we are told that Jesus is the atoning sacrifice, hilasmos, for the sins of the whole world. Hilasmos means the means of forgiveness.[15] It is explicitly stated that Christ is the means of forgiveness for the whole, holos, which means a totality as a complete unit, whole, entire,[16] world. The death of Jesus for the sins of the whole world is stated by John the Baptist when he said that Jesus is the Lamb of God who takes away the sin of the world (John 1:29). In 1 John 2:2 and John 1:29 *world*

---

[14]   *Ibid,* 288.

[15]   *Ibid,* 505.

[16]   *Ibid,* 597.

is from the Greek cosmos. Thus, the *all* of 1Timothy 2:6 is the whole, entire world; everyone.

The understanding that Jesus died for everyone is taught by Paul in 2 Corinthians 5:11-21. Paul, in this passage teaches that Christ died for all (2 Corinthians 5:14). In this passage the Greek word translated *for* means *for, on behalf of, for the sake of.*[17] The word *all* is from pas, which means *the totality of any object, mass or collective, all, every, each.*[18]The *all* that this passage refers to is all humanity. This is seen in 2 Corinthians 5:15 which states that the *all* from whom Christ died is divided into two categories. The first category is called *those who live.* The second category, by implication, is made up of those who do not live. Paul makes clear the teaching that Christ died for all in 2 Corinthians 5:18-21. In these verses Paul states that God has reconciled the *world*[19] to Himself through Christ (v. 18, 19). This statement agrees with Paul's previous statement that Christ died for all. Paul goes further and states that he was Christ's ambassador and as Christ's ambassador he was imploring people, that is those to whom God is now reconciled, to be reconciled to God (2 Corinthians 5:20). Paul makes

---

[17] *Ibid*, 802.

[18] *Ibid,* 597.

[19] World is from kosmos which means the universe and everything in it (Louw & Nida, *Greek-English Lexicon,* 1).

clear in this passage the teaching that although Christ died for all, not all will accept Christ and be saved when he writes that Christ died for all that we *might* become the righteousness of God (2 Corinthians 5:21). In this verse, *we might* become is in the subjunctive. The subjunctive is the mood of that which is conceivable.[20] This means that Paul wrote that it was conceivable that all might become the righteousness of God, but it was not a certainty that all would be. In 2 Corinthians 5:11-21 we see that God is reconciled to humanity; it is up to individuals, however, to be reconciled to God. Here again are the same two categories that Paul mentioned earlier in this passage.

What the Bible teaches then is that Jesus died as the means of forgiveness for everyone. The truth is while the offer of salvation is real and Christ truly died for the sins of everyone, not everyone will accept the offer of salvation and be saved (Revelation 2:21). The fact that not everyone will accept the Gospel does not mean that Jesus did not die for them nor does it mean that the offer of salvation is not genuine. Salvation is not automatic. Every individual must repent of his or her sin and accept for him or herself the grace of God in Christ Jesus. It is only then, that the death of Christ for that individual becomes reality for him or her.

---

[20] H. Dana & J. Mantey, *A Manual Grammar of Greek New Testament*, 170.

There are those who claim that if Jesus did die for everyone and everyone does not believe, then Jesus' death did not accomplish its whole purpose. In answer to this statement, the whole purpose of the death of Christ must be seen. The whole purpose of the death of Christ can be summed up in two main categories. Within each category there are multitudes of aspects concerning the death of Jesus. We will simply mention the main categories with a brief discussion concerning them. The first category is that Jesus died for sinners (1Timothy 2:6). The discussion for this category can be found above. The second main category is that Jesus died to cleanse creation, heaven included, from sin (Hebrews 9:23-28). Jesus came at the end of the ages for the purpose of doing away with sin (Hebrews 9:26). The doing away with sin includes the taking away of sin from people (Hebrews 9:28) and the cleansing of creation and heaven from sin (Hebrews 9:23-25). Sin has stained, has corrupted all of creation. The stench of sin reaches heaven itself (Genesis 18:20-21). Heaven and creation must be cleansed from sin. What is to be understood is that Jesus did not die just for individuals; although He did die for sinners. Jesus also died to cleanse heaven and earth from sin itself. Sin is not an isolated act; the stench of sin and sin itself reaches up to heaven itself (Ezra 9:6; Revelation 18:5). Jesus died to do away with sin completely throughout the creation. If Jesus did not die for everyone's sin, then, all of heaven and earth would not have been cleansed from sin. If there is one sin of one person that Jesus did not die for, then that sin and its corruption remains and heaven and the creation has not be cleansed from sin. Jesus is the answer to the problem, the existence, the stench of sin and not just the Savior of sinners. This does not mean of course, that every single person will eventually make it to heaven. Heaven is the home of the forgiven. While Jesus died for everyone's sin, each individual must repent and accept Jesus Christ as Lord and Savior to be forgiven and become a spiritual child of God.

When the Scripture is looked at, it will become clear that Jesus, the Second Adam, represented the whole human race and died for the whole human race. When this is added to Scriptural teaching regarding individuals representing a collective; what we are to understand is that Paul, in Romans 9 is referring not to individualistic election, but corporate election. While Paul is teaching corporate election, it is also important to understand that even in corporate election the eternal destinies of individual members of that collective are not determined by God.[21]

[21]   C.E.B. Cranfield, *The International Critical Commentary on Romans, Vol. 2* (Edinburgh: T & T Clark, 1979), 479.

In returning to Paul's discussion regarding Rebekah's twins; what Paul is teaching is that there is a difference between Israel as a race and Israel as the people of grace. The Israel of race and Israel of grace are not synonymous. God never promised to the race of Israel that they and they alone were the Israel of grace. In fact, the discussion of Paul in Romans clearly states that the Israel of grace, that is the people of grace, consists of those who have believed in the Lord Jesus Christ.

CHAPTER 2

HUMAN RESPONSIBILITY AND APOSTASY IN RELATION TO ELECTION

Last chapter it was stated that predestination/election was corporate and not individualistic. The main reason listed in chapter 1 for stating that election is corporate is that Paul claims in Romans election is corporate and not individualistic is the use of the individual for a collective.

In addition, this chapter will look at another reason that clearly states that predestination/election is not individualistic. If predestination/election were individualistic, then the destinies of individuals would be fixed and there would be nothing that they could do to alter that destiny. However, the teaching of Scripture is that the destiny of individuals is not fixed; each individual can choose for him or herself their eternal destiny.

There are two avenues that we will explore that state that people choose their own destinies. The first avenue is the many times throughout the Word of God where people are called to choose to obey or to suffer the consequences of their choice to disobey.

God, after leading the Hebrew people out of slavery in Egypt, assembled them together near the Jordan. The purpose of this assembly was to imprint on their hearts and minds that obedience to the Lord was essential. In addition, this assembly would also imprint on their hearts and minds that disobedience to God had catastrophic consequences.

The context of the assembly of the people was made up of the tribes of Israel separated into two groups. One group consisting of the tribes of Simeon, Levi, Judah, Issachar, Joseph and Benjamin were to stand on Mount Gerizim (Deuteronomy 27:12). The purpose of these particular tribes standing on Mount Gerizim was to pronounce God's blessings upon the people if they obeyed (Deuteronomy 27:12). The second group consisting of the tribes of Reuben, Gad, Asher, Zebulun, Dan and Naphalti were to stand of Mount Ebal. This second group while they stood on Mount Ebal, were to pronounce the curses that were the consequences of disobedience (Deuteronomy 27:13).

When the two groups were separated and standing upon the respective Mounts, the Levites were to recite to all the people of Israel curses with the people's response of agreement and commitment found in speaking the word *amen*[22] (Deuteronomy 27: 14-26). What is to be seen in

---

[22]   Amen has at its root the idea of certainty and assurance (R. Laird Harris, ed., *Theological Wordbook of the Old Testament, Vol.* I, Chicago: Moody Press, 1981, 51).

the people's response is the human choice and agreement to what follows.

After The Levites recited the curses and the people responded with agreement by saying *amen*; the Levites then announced the blessings of obeying the Lord and fully following His commands (Deuteronomy 28:1-14). After the blessings for obeying and fully following the Lord were recited and heard; the Levites then announced the curses for not obeying and for not fully following the Lord (Deuteronomy 28: 15-68).

The commitment to fully follow and obey the Lord was the covenant that He established with the people of Israel (Deuteronomy 29:1). The people of Israel, gathered before the Lord, were gathered as a sign that they had agreed with the terms of the covenant and were willing to enter into a relationship with God (Deuteronomy 29:12-15).

As Moses explained to the people of Israel the type of commitment that they were making he said: *Make sure that there is no man or woman, clan or tribe among you today whose heart turns away from the Lord our God* (Deuteronomy 29: 18). Moses went on to say that when a person hears the words of this oath that they were to not, even in the secret recesses of their heart or mind hold any part away from God; since even the secret things belong to God (Deuteronomy 29:19-29). In other words, the commitment that the people were to make with God was a commitment of their entire selves.

Moses then leads the people to a time of commitment to the Lord (Deuteronomy 30: 11-19). In this commitment, Moses tells the people that the relationship with God is not too difficult (Deuteronomy 30:11); nor is it beyond their ability to fully live out (Deuteronomy 30:11). Moses simply says that understanding, believing and obeying the covenant were not too much for them. The commitment to the covenant, to the Lord was in their hearts (Deuteronomy 30:14). Since the ability to obey the covenant was in their hearts; all that they needed to do was to express with their mouths, their words that they were entering this covenant relationship with God for the purpose of obeying and following the Lord (Deuteronomy 30:14).

Moses then leads the people to the point of making a commitment, a decision to follow God when he said: *See, I set before you today life and prosperity, death and destruction. If you love the Lord your God then you will live. But if your heart turns away and you are not obedient, you will be destroyed* (Deuteronomy 30: 15-18).

To ensure that the people of Israel understood the seriousness of choosing to obey or to disobey God, Moses then said that heaven and earth are witnesses that I have clearly stated the consequences of the two chooses that lay before the people in obedience or disobedience. Heaven and earth were not only witnesses that Moses set before the people obedience and disobedience and the consequences of each; but heaven and earth were witnesses against the people and the choice that they would make.

Moses then says: *choose life* (Deuteronomy 30:19). The word *choose* is bahar which always involves a careful, well thought-out choice and is used to express that choice which has eternal significance.[23]

When Joshua replaced Moses as God's representative to the people, he lead the people to renew the covenant that they had made under Moses. Joshua gaters the people at Shechem and recounts the acts of God on their behalf, beginning with their deliverance from Egypt to the time that they crossed the Jordan river into the Promised Land (Joshua 24: 1-13). Joshua then tells the people to fear the Lord and to serve Him with all faithfulness (Joshua 24:14). The word *fear* in this case is closely connected to proper living.[24] Joshua then goes on to say that if serving the Lord seems undesirable to you, the Hebrew literally is *evil in your eyes,* the people were to choose, bahar, whom they will serve (Joshua 24:15).

When Solomon had finished the temple of the Lord, the Lord appeared to him and said: *If my people, who*

---

[23] Harris, *Theological Wordbook of the Old Testament, Vol. I,* 100.

[24] *Ibid,* 400.

are called by my name, will humble themselves and pray and seek, (with the idea of desiring[25]) *my face and turn* (the word turn is from *shub.* Shub both sums up human responsibility in the process of repentance, such as: "incline your heart to the Lord (Joshua 24:23); circumcise yourselves to the Lord (Jeremiah 4:4); wash your heart from wickedness (Jeremiah 4:14); and combines in its meaning the two requirements of repentance: to turn from evil and to turn to the good.[26] In addition, shub, to return is also understood as conversion[27] *from their wicked ways, then I will hear from heaven, forgive their sin and will heal their land* (2 Chronicles 7:14).

The teaching of human choice when faced with the Gospel is taught by Jesus as well. He said: *If anyone chooses to do God's will* (NIV), that one will find out whether His teaching comes from God or not (John 7:17). By the word *if* Jesus used what is called a conditional sentence. This type of conditional sentence is used in situations where the speaker expresses a degree of uncertainty as to fulfillment of the condition.[28] A second

---

[25] Ibid, *126.*

[26] Harris, *Theological Wordbook of the Old Testament, Vol. II,* 909.

[27] R. Girdlestone, *Synonyms of the Old Testament* (Grand Rapids: Eerdmans, 1981), 92.

[28] H. E. Dana & J. Mantey, *A Manual Grammar of the Greek New Testament* (New York: MacMillan, 1957), 288.

fact that describes uncertainty or doubt in the condition is the use of the subjunctive mood. The subjunctive is used when there is doubt in the mind of the speaker as to the realization of his or her words.[29] Jesus, by the use of the particular type of conditional clause and the subjunctive mood placed the responsibility of the *choosing* on people themselves as is made clear in the use of the word thelo, which means to choose, to desire, to want.[30]

Paul, echoing the teaching of Jesus exhorts people to be reconciled with God (2 Corinthians 5: 20). In this passage, Paul states that he is Christ's ambassador and through him, God was making his appeal. This appeal, made on Christ's behalf which means as if Christ Himself was making it, is: be reconciled to God.

In this passage there is found urgencies in the Gospel message. The first urgency is found in the word *implores*. As the ambassador of Christ, Paul implores, deomai, which means to ask for with urgency, to beg.[31] Paul, speaking for Christ Himself is passionate in his presentation of the Gospel and in urging individuals to respond. The second urgency found in this passage is seen to be an urgency within the heart of God Himself. Paul states that God is making his appeal through him. In this passage, the word

---

[29]   *Ibid,* 170.

[30]   Louw & Nida, *Greek-English Lexicon,* 289.

[31]   *Ibid,* 408.

appeal can be understood to mean: to ask for something earnestly, to plead, earnest request.[32] Thus, we understand that God through Paul is pleading that individuals would respond to the Gospel and to be reconciled to God. The Greek form of the word, *be reconciled* is imperative. The imperative is the form by which a command is made.[33] In addition, the essence of the imperative is that it is an appeal from one will to another.[34]

Christ, through Paul, was pleading, begging people to respond to the Gospel and to be reconciled with God. There is clearly seen in this passage both God's intentions/decrees and human responsibility.

The second avenue that we will explore in this chapter that states that people can choose their own destiny is the clear teaching of people's choice found in the teaching of apostasy. The teaching concerning apostasy says that individuals' destinies are not fixed.

The destiny of individuals, predestination/election must be seen in light of the teaching regarding apostasy or what is called losing one's salvation. This chapter will look at the question: Can a Christian commit apostasy? The word apostasy is defined as: To at one time believe

---

[32] *Ibid,* 408.

[33] Dana & Mantey, *A Manual Grammar of the Greek New Testament*, 174.

[34] *Ibid,* 174.

in Christ, be saved and then to no longer believe in Jesus Christ and thus be lost. This question has divided the Christian Church for a long time. In fact, this question has not only divided Christians but there is a chasm in the minds of some Christians that cannot be crossed. This chasm divides, in the perspective of some, True Christians from Non-Christians and the ones on the other side of the chasm are not even in Christ. This claim is made regardless of the life and commitment of the others. This question, in the mind of some has become *the* question whether a person is truly a Christian or not. We will look at Scripture passages to discover the meaning that is found in the Bible, the Word of God in regards to this question. In the previous chapters we looked at what it means to be saved and we will repeat some of that in this chapter. Our purpose will be to attempt to answer the question of the possibility of apostasy for Christians.

The following passages will be listed and discussed to discover the teaching included within them concerning the possibility of apostasy.

Isaiah 24:5—states that it is possible to break God's everlasting covenant.

John 12:48—In this passage, Jesus clearly teaches that it is possible to accept and to reject Him. The human race is not mere drift wood being tossed to and fro on the whim of God's decrees. God has not determined beforehand who will accept and who will reject Christ. Jesus said that the one who hears His words and does not believe in Him rejects both Jesus and the Father. The key in this passage is that Jesus spoke His words to all who would listen. Those who accepted His words were given light (John 12:44-46). The one who hears Jesus' words, but does not believe in Him chooses judgment (John 12:47, 48).

John 15:6-Jesus said that it is possible to be *in Him*, that is to be in the Branch, at one time, become fruitless and then be cut off by the Father (John 15:2), cast into the fire and be burned (John 15:6). A deeper discussion of the word *fire* that Jesus referred to in this verse, will be conducted later on in this chapter. At this point, we notice that Jesus, by His following words makes two statements of truth. The first truth is that it is possible to remain in Christ and to live a fruitful life (John 15:7). The second truth is seen in the conditional clause introduced by *if* at the beginning of the verse and in the mood of the verse used in John 15:7. In conditional clauses, the mood of the word *if* describes the amount of certainty or doubt as to the fulfillment of the condition.[35] The conditional clause in John 15:7 is introduced by ean. ean is used in conditions where the speaker expresses a degree of uncertainty as to fulfillment of the condition.[36] A second fact that describes

---

[35]   *Ibid*, 287.

[36]   *Ibid*, 288.

uncertainty or doubt in the condition is the use of the subjunctive mood in John 15:7. The subjunctive is used when there is doubt in the mind of the speaker as to the realization of his or her words.[37] Jesus, by the use of the particular type of conditional clause and the subjunctive mood expressed a degree of uncertainty as to whether all of His followers would remain in Him. It is possible to state the same thing from a different perspective and that is; Jesus by the use of the subjunctive mood and the particular type of conditional clause made it known that there is the possibility that some of His followers might not remain in Him.

Romans 11:11—In this passage Paul is discussing the situation with the Jewish people, those who at the time of the writing of the letter to the Romans had not believed in Jesus Christ. Paul asks: did they fall beyond recovery? The understanding was that the covenants given by God to Israel are eternal covenants (Judges 2:1). Has God rejected Israel, is that the end of Israel, Paul asks? Within the question itself is Paul's answer. Paul uses may in his asking the question. The Greek word is used in a question when the answer is *no*.[38] Israel and her experience is an example for Christians. If Israel can receive the blessings of God which are eternal and turn

---

[37]   *Ibid,* 170.

[38]   *Ibid,* 265.

from God, it is possible also for Christians to receive the Holy Spirit, be saved (Hebrews 6:4-6) and then turn from God. When Christians turn from God, they reject Jesus Christ and are thus lost.

Romans 11:20-23—Paul is discussing the relationship of the Jews to salvation. He states that many of the Jewish people fell because of unbelief (Romans 11:20) and were thus broken off of the root (Romans 11:18). The idea behind the word *fell* is to cease, to stop.[39] The Jews fell from salvation because they stopped believing. He goes on to warn the believers who came out of the Gentile peoples to remain in belief. If they do not continue in belief they too will be cut off (Romans 11:22). To be cut off means to be cut in such a way as to cause separation.[40] This verb is used in Matthew 3:10 to describe the cutting off/down of trees that do not bear good fruit. These trees will then be cast into the fire. Matthew 3:10 refers to producing good fruit for God (Matthew 3:7-10).

Galatians 5:4—Paul, in this passage is writing to Christians (Galatians 3:15, 26; 4:8, 9, 12; 5:1 where Paul addresses the recipients and himself as *us*). He states that the recipients had been running a good race of faith (Galatians 5:7), yet, someone had hindered their

---

[39]   J. Louw & E, Nida, *A Greek-English Lexicon of the New Testament,* 661.

[40]   *Ibid,* 225.

progress and kept them from obeying the truth. A point to notice is that faith in Christ is the truth. All attempts to be right with God other than by faith in Jesus Christ are not the truth but a lie, a false way. Paul states to the believers that at one time they were in faith, but by being circumcised they had fallen from grace, ekpipto, which means to abandon a former relationship.[41] The key words are *former relationship*. The meaning is that at one time the recipients did have a relationship with Christ in grace. However, to turn to the Law was to reject Christ and to fall from grace, which clearly means to no longer be in grace, to no longer have a relationship with Christ. To have a former relationship with someone or something means that the relationship no longer exists. A former relationship clearly expresses the fact that at one time a relationship existed but now no longer exists. It is simply not possible to have a former relationship with Christ without the possibility of leaving that relationship.

Colossians 1:23—Paul states that the Colossian Christians would be presented before God holy, without blemish and free from accusation *if* they continued in their faith and if they were not moved, metakineo, which contains the idea of the complete cessation of a state,[42] from the hope of the Gospel. The idea behind the word

---

[41]   *Ibid,* 449.

[42]   *Ibid,* 154.

state is a relationship, a way of being. The relationship in this context is with the Gospel. In other words, the Colossian Christians had a relationship with the Gospel, with Jesus Christ that it was possible to move from. The complete cessation of a state means that the state at one time existed, but now no longer does.

1Timothy 1:19-20—Paul writes to Timothy and exhorts him to hold on to faith and a good conscience. He then says to Timothy that there are some who have rejected faith and thus a good conscience. He mentions Hymenaeus and Alexander as two examples (1 Timothy 1:20). We begin our investigation of this passage with the definition of *rejected*. Rejected is from apotheomai with the meaning to reject in the sense of no longer paying attention to previous beliefs.[43] Hymenaeus and Alexander rejected previously held beliefs and thus shipwrecked their faith (1Timothy 19).

1Timothy 2:15—Paul states that if someone remains, meno, which means to remain, to continue in activity or state,[44] in faith. The word *if* is *ean* which is used to indicate uncertainty and is therefore not used when there is certainty about something.[45] The question, the

---

[43]   *Ibid*, 374.

[44]   *Ibid*, 656.

[45]   H. Dana & J. Mantey, *A Manual Grammar of the Greek New Testament*, 245.

uncertainty in Paul's mind is whether the people he is addressing will remain in faith. If Paul is not certain that they will remain in faith, there must be the possibility of not remaining in faith. To not remain in faith means that at one time someone was in faith but is now no longer. One cannot be said to not remain in faith if one was not at one time in faith.

1 Timothy 4:1—Paul writes that the Holy Spirit says that in the last days there will be those who abandon, *aphistamai*, which means to move away from with emphasis upon separation and the lack of concern for what has been left.[46] The *Holy Spirit* says that in the later times there will be those who abandon, forsake[47] the faith. To abandon, forsake, to separate from the faith means that at one time there was a relationship with faith. It is not possible to abandon faith if one only professes the faith but never possesses the faith. To abandon the faith means that at one time one possessed the faith. What is also significant in the discussion concerning whether apostasy is a Biblical teaching is that in this verse it is God who says that there exists the possibility of apostasy, of rejecting grace and falling from a previous relationship

---

[46] J. Louw & E. Nida, *Greek-English Lexicon of the New Testament,* 189.

[47] To abandon, to forsake are further shades of meaning of ajfivstamai, J. Louw & E. Nida, *Greek-English Lexicon of the New Testament,* 449.

with Jesus Christ. It is God in the Holy Spirit who says that the possibility exists for a Christian to be able to move away from Christ and to finally reject Him and thus no longer being in grace, which means that the person was saved but is no longer saved.

1 Timothy 5: 8—The first point to understand is that Paul is writing about Christians who do not provide for their relatives. We know that Paul is referring to a Christian because Paul says that the Christian who does not provide for his family is worse than an unbeliever. The second point to notice is that the Christian who does not provide for his family has denied, *arneomai*, which carries the meaning of to deny any relationship with, the faith. When Paul writes that when a Christian does not provide for his or her family that Christian has denied that he or she has any relationship with the faith. This means that a Christian is able to live in such a way as to distance him or herself from the faith. While it is true that the situation just described does not necessarily mean that the Christian in question has rejected Christ. It may simply mean that the Christian in question is living a life of sin, which in essence is a rejection of God and His Word. However, a caution must be issued at this point. While it is true this verse may not describe a Christian who has rejected Christ, it is to be understood that the same verb used in this verse is used in Matthew 10:33 where Jesus says that if anyone denies me before others, that He will deny them before the Father.

1Timothy 6:10-In this verse there are two statements that prove the truthfulness of each other. The first statement is that the love of money is the root of all evil. This is such a common truth that it is not difficult to prove. All one has to do is look around them and notice what people will do for money. People will sell themselves; they will lie, kill, steal and much more all to gain money. Now, recognizing the truth that the love of money is the root of all evil; we turn to the second statement in this verse which is proven to be true by the truthfulness of the first statement. The second statement is that some Christians have fallen in love with money that they have wandered from the faith. Wandered from the truth is from *apoplanamai* which means to no longer believe what is true and to start believing what is false.[48] The Christians who have fallen in love with money have wandered *from*, apo, implying a rupture from a former association,[49] the faith (1 Timothy 6:10). These Christians were at one time in the faith, for they wandered from the faith, in the sense that their former relationship with faith has been severed. It is not possible to sever an imaginary connection; thus the Christians referred to by Paul, at one time, had a real

---

[48]   *Ibid,* 374.

[49]   *Ibid,* 794.

relationship with Christ by faith and for the love of money destroyed their relationship with Christ.

1 Timothy 6: 20, 21—Timothy is exhorted to guard what was entrusted to him by turning away from godless chatter and certain opposing ideas that is falsely called knowledge. Paul then goes on to say that there are some who have embraced this so-called knowledge and have wandered from the faith. To wander from the faith is from *astocheo*, which means to go astray as the result of departing from the truth.[50] One cannot depart from the truth unless one has been in the truth.

2 Timothy 2:17, 18—In this passage, Paul mentions Hymenaeus and Philetus who had wandered from the truth, *astocheo*, which means to go astray as the result of departing from the truth; to abandon.[51] One cannot depart from something unless one is at, in the something which is departed from. The truth is not simply a certain set of doctrinal teaching; the truth is Jesus Christ (John 14:6). Thus to wander from the truth is to wander from Christ. Their departure from the truth is seen in their teaching that the resurrection had already taken place.

Hebrews 3:12, 13—In this passage, the writer to the Hebrews is exhorting his brethren (Hebrews 3:12); so we know that he is addressing Christians. The recipients of

---

[50]   *Ibid,* 374.

[51]   *Ibid,* 374.

the letter to the Hebrews are told to watch their hearts. It is in the guarding of one's heart that an evil, unbelieving heart is not allowed to come into existence. When one's heart becomes an evil, unbelieving heart; that person has turned from the Living God. The words *turned from* is *aphistamai*, which means to abandon a former relationship.[52] The key word in this definition is *former*. To turn from the Living God implies that one had, at one time, a relationship with the Living God. It is impossible to turn from, to abandon one's relationship with the Living God if one has never had a relationship with the Living God. It is this Greek word that we get the English *apostasy*. It is clearly stated in this passage that a Christian can become so enamored by sin that his or her heart becomes calloused and hardened to the voice of the Holy Spirit urging the Christian to return to the Way. Eventually, if a Christian's heart is not softened by grace; that Christian will turn from the Living God. In this passage, the writer to the Hebrews tells plainly how to keep from apostasy; from turning from the Living God. It is in the encouraging one another and the being encouraged by other Christians, which implies an active involvement in a Christian fellowship, that one is protected from being hardened by sin's deceitfulness (Hebrews 3:13).

---

[52]   *Ibid,* 449.

Hebrews 6:4-6—This passage has generated much debate in the Church. There are those who say that what the writer to the Hebrews is saying is impossible, that it is a *straw man*. By straw man, those who say this mean that the writer to the Hebrews is stating a case that cannot in any manner occur. Another view of this passage is that the ones being describe only *professed* the Christian faith and a commitment to Christ. In this position, the meaning behind the word professed is that the ones being described never actually *possessed* Christ nor experienced conversion or salvation. A third view is that this passage refers to Christians who reject Christ and fall from grace.

We begin our exploration of this passage by observing that the English *enlightened, tasted, shared,* all describe the people being referred to. These characteristics are important to understand. The writer to the Hebrews uses the phrase *enlightened* again in 10:32 to describe the previous commitment of the recipients to Christ. The Greek translated *enlightened* is also used in Luke 11:36 to describe the filling of the person with light and the driving away of all darkness. This verb is also used in John 1:9 to describe the ministry of Jesus Christ who came into the world to bring light to all people. This verb is again used in 1 Corinthians 4:5 to describe the work of Jesus when He brings to light, makes known all secrets. Paul uses this verb in Ephesians 1:18 to describe the work of the

Holy Spirit in opening the understanding of the people to the hope given to them by Jesus. Again, Paul uses this verb to describe the making known of the mystery which God kept hidden for ages (Ephesians 3:9). Paul, in writing to Timothy, uses this verb to describe in part the work of Christ when Paul says that Jesus brings life and immortality to light through the Gospel (2 Timothy1:10). This verb is also used to describe the illumination of the earth by an angel (Revelation 18:1). This verb is used again in Revelation to describe how the glory of God covers and illumines the whole world (Revelation 21:23). Finally, this verb is used in Revelation 22:5 to describe the work of God in giving light to all His followers.

To enlighten is the work of God in Christ Jesus through the Holy Spirit. This work can be divided into two categories. The first category is that Jesus, when He came into the world enlightened all people (John 1:9). This meaning is seen in the phrase all men of John 1:9. The use of the singular and not the plural indicates that every person individually has received the beginning of the light.[53] Every person understands to a small degree, but until they believe they do not fully know.[54] We certainly are not saying that all people have received the Holy

---

[53] L. Morris, *The Gospel According to John* (Grand Rapids: Eerdmans, 1981), 94.

[54] G. Osborne, *Romans*, 47.

Spirit. Only those who have accepted Jesus Christ as Lord and Savior have received the Holy Spirit (Romans 8:9). The Bible tells us that Jesus gives the Light to those who believe in Him (John 3:19-21). This is true. However, the Bible also tells us that God has revealed something about Himself to all people everywhere (Romans 1:20). This something is the faint light that Jesus has brought into the world and which all people have experienced. The light, the grace of God, was given in the world and which all people have encountered in a beginning degree. The grace of God is not a something; it is the very presence of God. The experience of grace that all people have encountered is not the experience of salvation; but this experience of grace restores the ability of everyone to say yes or no to Christ and the claims of the Gospel.[55] It is this experience of grace; this encounter with the presence of God that was rejected by the world.[56] We know that grace, the presence of God was in the world since creation (Genesis 1:2). In addition to the Holy Spirit's presence in the world; creation itself was accomplished by the Word of God, Jesus Christ. In the act, the work of creation, God spoke and it came into existence (Genesis 1:3ff). This speaking

---

[55] J. Wesley, *Explanatory Notes Upon the New Testament, Vol. I* (Kansas City: Beacon Hill Press, 1983).

[56] R. Kysar, *John* (Minneapolis: Augsburg Publishing House, 1986), 31.

by God was a creative act and an implanting, a giving a part of Himself into the world (Romans 1:20). The second category is the enlightening which the believers in Christ experience (John 3:19-21). This enlightening begins when an individual accepts Jesus Christ as Lord and Savior but continues into the future. Also, individual Christians will receive the amount of light based upon their faithfulness and commitment to Jesus Christ. Thus, while it is true that every Christian has received the light; it is also true that some Christians experience more of the light than other Christians.

The word *tasted* is the second of the words that are characteristics of certain people. This word is used in reference to *tasting the heavenly gift.* There are some who say this simply refers to those who have taken communion, the Eucharist. However, Jesus described Himself as the gift of God (John 4:10). Peter calls the Holy Spirit the gift of God (Acts 2:38). Paul makes mention of the gift of grace and of righteousness in Romans 5:15, 17 and associates these gifts with the person of Jesus Christ. *Tasted* is also used to describe the relationship, the experience that these people had with the Word of God and the powers of the coming age. The phrase *the coming age* is used by Jesus to describe the fact that those who sins against the Holy Spirit will not experience forgiveness either in this present age or in the *coming age.*

The third word *shared* is used to describe a relationship with the Holy Spirit. To share in the Holy Spirit means that the person involved has received the Holy Spirit. This is seen in the Greek that is translated *share.* The Greek literally means to *become a companion, partner* of the Holy Spirit. The word translated *companion, partner* is *metochos* which means one who shares with someone else as an associate in an undertaking.[57] An important understanding in this is that only a Christian has received the Holy Spirit (Romans 8:9) which means that only a Christian can share in the Holy Spirit.

What we are to understand is that the writer to the Hebrews is describing experiences that not only every Christian has, but these experiences belong *only* to Christians. This is the case, for only a Christian can share in the Holy Spirit. The objection to these experiences belonging to Christians falls short when it is known that Paul himself taught that Christians can fall from grace. This is seen in Galatians 3:2-14 where Paul says that it is possible to receive the Holy Spirit by faith (Galatians 3:2) and then by the rejection of grace becoming cursed by God (Galatians 3:10). There were some in the church at Galatia who, after beginning their relationship with Christ by faith, then, began to turn to the Law as the means by

---

[57]   J. Louw & E. Nida, *Greek-English Lexicon of the New Testament,* 447.

which they were acceptable to God. To become cursed by God is to no longer be in grace.

Paul expounds on the possibility of falling from grace in Galatians 5:4. In this passage, Paul is addressing the Christians at Galatia who have listened to and are leaning towards the teaching of the ones who said that believing in Jesus was enabled a person to stand before God's throne. This teaching then went on to state that the Judgment of God was based on how one kept the Law. Because the Christians at Galatia were beginning to believe this teaching, Paul told them very clearly that if they were circumcised, they were then obligated to keep the whole law (Galatians 5:3). What is fundamental to this passage is the teaching of the Bible that the Law was never given to bring justification, sanctification or God's blessings (Galatians 3:19-25). The Law was never given by God for any purpose other than to teach what sin is (Galatians 3: 19-22) and to lead people to faith in Jesus Christ (Galatians 3:22-25). The plain teaching of the Bible is that the Law was not, is not and will never be the basis for salvation or used by God as the basis for judgment. The Law is not the basis upon which God accepts or rejects anyone.

In the mind of those who base their future glory on the Law, the Law has become the basis of acceptance with God. The Law is thus a competitor with Jesus Christ and grace. We must understand that if acceptance by

God is based on the Law, then grace and faith have no meaning. The fact is the Law was never given as a means of acceptance with God (Galatians 3:15-25). Acceptance with God, which is termed righteousness is in Jesus Christ and is a gift of grace which is received by faith (Ephesians 2:8, 9). If the Law is the basis for acceptance with God, then works, human effort, becomes the basis for salvation, sanctification and glorification. If that is the case, then Christ died for nothing. If someone bases their future on the Law, that person does not have a relationship with Jesus Christ, even if that person thinks that they do have a relationship with Christ (Galatians 5:2).

The fundamental statement of Paul's opposition to the Law as the basis for acceptance with God and of God's blessings is that if a person tries to be right with God, the word for right with God is justification, that person has fallen from grace (Galatians 5:4). We begin this discussion with a definition of justification. Justification is the term that scholars use to describe the initial experience that a believing person has with Jesus Christ. In the understanding of these scholars, justification is synonymous with regeneration, the new birth and conversion. While it is true that justification is used at times for the initial experience of salvation; justification is also used for more. Justification is from *dikaioo* which means to cause someone to be in a right relationship with someone.[58] While *dikaioo* is translated justification in most cases in the New Testament and is thus used for the initial step of salvation, *dikaioo* also has several shades of meaning. *dikaioo* is used to describe being set free morally from the control of something or some situation.[59] *dikaioo* also refers to the conforming to righteous and just commands.[60] Finally, *dikaioo* at times is used for the act of clearing someone from transgression, which means to remove guilt.[61] What we are to understand from the various shades of meaning is that *dikaioo* is used at times in the New Testament for more than the initial step of salvation. *dikaioo* can be said to cover the entire spectrum of a person's relationship with God. We return to Galatians 5:4 where Paul states that if a person tries to be right with God, dikaioo, at any point in both time, now and before God's judgment throne; and also at any time in that person's relationship with God, that person has fallen from grace.

A very interesting phrase is *fallen from grace*. Grace is the very basis of God's relating to His creation.[62] There never has been a time when God related to creation in

---

[58]   *Ibid,* 452.

[59]   *Ibid,* 489.

[60]   *Ibid,* 468.

[61]   *Ibid,* 557.

[62]   R. Trench, *Synonyms of the New Testament* (Grand Rapids: Eerdmans, 1980), 168.

anyway other than grace.[63] Grace is also the atmosphere, the very fabric and totality of God's creation. Grace is the very medium, the means by which God has any favorable view of anyone.[64] Grace refers to the restored harmonious relationship between God and human beings.[65] Grace is the typical quality of the age to come.[66] Grace is thus to be seen as the very basis for and the relationship itself between God and His creation. To fall from grace is a very serious act. What we are to understand is, if someone lives in a fallen state, that person is outside of God's favor; that person can in no way please God at all. To fall from grace means that one has no relationship at all with God. To fall from grace means that a person is no longer in God's sphere, God's world; but the one who has fallen from grace is in the world in the sense of that sphere, that mentality, that relationship that is in opposition to God. To fall from grace means that a person is no longer a friend of God but is now an enemy of God.

---

[63] Girdlestone, Synonyms of the Old Testament, 107.

[64] J. Louw & E. Nida, Greek-English Lexicon of the New Testament, 299.

[65] J. Moulton & G. Milligan, The Vocabulary of the Greek New Testament (Grand Rapids: Eerdmans, 1982), 685.

[66] W. Ardnt & F. W. Gingrich, A Greek-English Lexicon of the New Testament and Other Early Christian Literature (Chicago: The University of Chicago Press, 1979), 878.

Paul said that if a person attempts to be right in anyway and at any time by the Law, that person has fallen from grace. The phrase to fall from grace means that a person has been in grace at one time and is now no longer in grace. To fall from grace states clearly that at one time the fallen from grace person lived in grace and had a relationship with God; but now no longer has a relationship with God. The reason that the attempt to be right with God; to be accepted by God, by the Law causes one to fall from grace is that the Law was never given as a means of being acceptable to God; of being right with God (Galatians 3:11). The Law was given that the human race might know what sin is (Romans 5:20). The Law had the purpose of leading people to faith in Christ (Galatians 3:24). The Law was, is and will always be a means to an end; that end is faith in Christ. A person, who in their mind, attempts to be right with God is a person outside of the God-given means of acceptance. The God-given means of acceptance is grace through faith (Ephesians 2:8, 9). Thus, for a person to attempt to be right with God by the way they live, which is an attempt at acceptance with God by living right, that person is outside of God's means of salvation, which is faith through grace. To be outside of grace is to no longer be in grace. To have been, at one time in grace and then to no longer be in grace is to have fallen from grace.

We return to Hebrews 6:4-6 and the words *enlightened, tasted* and *shared* to understand that the writer to the Hebrews is describing real people and real events. The first point to notice is that these words in the Greek are articular aorist participles. It is stated in the Greek grammars that participles in the Greek New Testament are used to describe action as real.[67] This means that what the writer to the Hebrews is describing is the real experiences. A second point to notice is that all these participles are articular participles. The definite article is found in Hebrews 6:4 and modifies all the aorist participles in this passage. We know this because the definite article is masculine accusative plural and all the aorist participles are masculine accusative plural. An articular participle is simply a participle that is modified by the article, which is usually the definite article, the word *the*. So, what we have in Hebrews 6:4-6 are participles that are modified by the word *the*. The participle with its modifiers, in this case, *the,* describe what person is being referred to.[68] In other words, real people and real experiences are being described and not an unreal idea or straw man. Thus we are lead to this conclusion that these participles are not

---

[67] H. Dana & J. Mantey, *A Manual Grammar of the Greek New Testament*, 222.

[68] J. Machen, *New Testament Greek for Beginners* (Toronto: MacMillan, 1951), 108.

describing those people who profess to be Christian but do not possess true salvation. The articular participles used in this passage describe real people who had real experiences with the Holy Spirit, yet, at some point turned from grace, from Christ.

We know that some of the people the writer to the Hebrews is describing turned from grace because we are told exactly that. The writer to the Hebrews states that *if they fall away* (Hebrews 6:6). We notice that *fall away* is also an aorist participle modified by the same, *the,* as the other aorist participles in this passage. Because the participle translated *fall away* is modified by the same definite article as the other aorist participles in this passage, we are lead to the conclusion that all of the aorist participles in this passage describe the same people.

We now want to know what is meant by *fall away.* Fall away is *parapipto* which means to abandon a former relationship.[69] We look first of all at the word *former.* The word *former* implies that something a person once had, that person no longer possesses. In other words, if one is to abandon a *former* relationship, it is obvious that one has to have that particular relationship previously. One cannot abandon a particular relationship if one has never had that relationship. Secondly we notice that *fall away*

---

[69] J. Louw & E. Nida, *Greek-English Lexicon of the New Testament,* 449.

means to abandon a former relationship. Abandon means to forsake. If one is to abandon something or someone, the other thing or person must be someone or something in which one has a relationship with. You cannot abandon something or someone that you were not at some point in time related to.

Thus, we are lead to understand that this passage does not refer to someone who only appears to have accepted Christ nor does it refer to a straw man. A further reason for rejecting the idea of a straw man is that the text of Hebrews 6:4-6 in no way includes either the phrase *straw man* nor does it teach the idea of a straw man. Hebrews 6:4-6 must refer to people who have truly accepted Christ, were born-again and for some reason rejected Christ and because of the rejection of Christ have fallen from grace.

Hebrews 10:26-29—If we deliberately keep on sinning after we have received the knowledge of the truth. If we deliberately keep on sinning after we have *received,* lambano, the knowledge of the truth. *Lambano* means to receive or accept an abject or benefit for which the initiative rests with the giver, but the focus of attention in the transfer is upon the receiver, to receive, to accept.[70] In the word *received* we see the teaching that the person in question has indeed accepted the knowledge of the truth. If *we* deliberately keep on sinning after we have received

---

[70]   *Ibid,* 572.

the knowledge of the truth. The writer to the Hebrews is not talking about some figment of the imagination, a non-real person or situation. The writer says if *we*, he is addressing the recipients of the letter, who are Christians and he is including himself in the group of those for whom it is possible to receive the truth and afterwards deliberately sin. If we deliberately keep on sinning after we have received the knowledge of the truth. The word *deliberately* is *hekousious* which has the meaning of being willing to do something without being forced or pressured, willing.[71] The teaching here is of choice to sin; a willingness, a wanting to sin. The writer to the Hebrews is not addressing the Christian who stumbles and sins, but does so with a heart that wants to please the Lord Jesus. The writer to the Hebrews is addressing those who have made a deliberate choice of turning to sin from God. This is seen in Hebrews 10:29 where the deliberate sin is described. The idea behind the deliberate sin is an utter disdain for the Son of God; a trampling, a despising of the very person and work of Jesus Christ.[72] The deliberate sin of Hebrews 10:26 is also a considering as unholy, as something to be avoided, the blood of Jesus and His redeeming work. It is to be clearly seen that the *we*

---

[71]   Ibid, 296.

[72]   See the meaning of katapateo in J. Louw & E. Nida, *Greek-English Lexicon of the New Testament*, 763.

of Hebrews 10:26 are Christians. This is seen in the fact the ones who despise both Jesus and His redeeming work have been sanctified by the blood of Jesus Christ (Hebrews 10:29). The deliberate sin of Hebrews 10:26 is the sin of apostasy; it is not the stumbling of the Christian who wants to please the Lord Jesus in all things. What will happen to those Christians who reject Christ and His redeeming blood? We are told that they will be punished by God (Hebrews 10:29). The punishment referred to here is not the slapping of the wrist by God at the Day of Judgment for the Christian. The Day of Judgment for the Christian will not be a day of punishment but of a recognizing of the Christian's times of obedience and faithfulness. There will be no punishment for the Christian (1 John 4:18). In John 4:18 *punishment,* kolasis is used in Matthew 25:46 to describe the eternal punishment in store for those who do not obey the Lord Jesus. The Christian, however, is in no danger of condemnation or punishment (Romans 8:1). In Romans 8:1 the word for *condemnation* is *katakrima* which means to judge someone as guilty and thus subject to punishment.[73] There is no condemnation or punishment for the Christian. Thus, Hebrews 10:26-29, the writer to the Hebrews, while addressing Christians, states very clearly that it is possible for the Christian to leave grace

---

[73]   *Ibid,* 556.

and thus be liable to punishment by committing deliberate sin, which is apostasy.

James 5:19—In this verse, James states that to help a wandering, *planaomai* which means to no longer believe what is true and to start believing what is false,[74] Christian return to the truth covers a multitude of sins. We are told clearly that it is possible for a Christian to wander from the truth; that is to no longer believe that Jesus is the truth. We digress a bit here to define what the New Testament says is faith. There are Christians who hold to the understanding of faith as the believing, the holding of correct Christian doctrines. However, the New Testament does not teach that view. The New Testament teaches that faith is not the hearing of the Gospel; nor is faith simply the holding to correct Christian doctrines. We are told that the demons know intellectually the truth in a clearer way than we Christians do, yet, the intellectual holding to correct Christian doctrines is not enough to save the demons (James 2:18, 19). If the mere holding to correct Christian doctrines put the demons in the position of shuddering or fearing, it will do the same for human beings. We see this in the fact that the mere holding to correct Christian doctrines leads not to salvation but to the mere cluttering of the mind with information. The holding to correct Christian doctrines alone is death (James 2:17);

---

[74]   *Ibid,* 374.

it is not life; it is not salvation. There are others within the Christian Church that hold to the view that faith is the lifestyle of working for social justice, however, the New Testament does not agree with this view either. The New Testament teaches that it is possible to perform, to do, to live a life of social justice and do it without God (1 Corinthians 13). 1 Corinthians 13 is called the love chapter; yet, when one reads this passage of Scripture, one sees that it is possible to speak in tongues without love, it is possible to be prophetic without love, that it is possible to move mountains and do this without love, that it is possible to live a life of working for social justice by giving one's possessions to the poor, giving one's body to the fire and to do it all without love. Love is not a mere sentiment. God is love (1 John 4:16) and love comes from God (1 John 4:7). Thus, to live a life working for social justice is possible to be done without God; which is also without faith. Faith is not the mere holding to correct Christian doctrines, for even the demons know the truth. Faith is also not the life spent in service to others. Faith is both holding to the correct doctrine and a life lived out in service to God and neighbor (Galatians 5:6).

2 Peter 2:20-22—Peter writes that it is possible to escape the corruption of the world by the indwelling of God's Spirit (2 Peter 1:4). In this statement, Peter is referring to Christians. This is seen in the fact that only a Christian has the Holy Spirit indwelling them (Romans 8:9) and that Peter states that those who have escaped the corruption of the world have done it through knowing Jesus Christ as Lord and Savior (2 Peter 2:20). Jesus calls escaping the corruption of the world through a spiritual relationship with Himself; being born-again (John 3:3). Peter says that it is possible, for those who have escaped the corruption of the world to become entangled in the corruption of the world once again (2 Peter 2:20). What is informative is Peter's description of what takes place for a person to become a Christian. Peter describes becoming a Christian as an escape from the corruption of the world through the indwelling of the Holy Spirit. He then adds that it is possible for a Christian that is one who has at one time escaped the corruption of the world, to become once again entangled in the corruption of the world. Peter says that for a Christian to once again become entangled in the corruption of the world after he or she has received the Holy Spirit, that person has turned his or her back on the sacred command given and has returned to the mud, the mire, the world itself (2 Peter 2:21, 22).

2 Peter 3:17—In this passage, Peter is making clear that the writings of Paul are part of the Scriptures, the Word of God (2 Peter 3:14-17). Peter emphasizes the fact that, although Paul's writings are hard to understand, it is important that Christians pay attention to Paul's writings and to not listen to the errors of lawless teachers (2 Peter 3:17). In the understanding of Peter, to turn one's back on the Scriptures and to listen to the errors of lawless, that is to listen to Non-Christian teachers, is to fall from one's secure position (2 Peter 3:17). To fall from means to abandon a former relationship, to fall away.[75] The secure position that Peter refers to is a state of security and safety.[76] This secure position is both a place and an inner commitment.[77] There is only one secure position and that position is salvation (2 Peter 3:15) resulting in growth in the grace and knowledge of the Lord Jesus (2 Peter 3:18). Thus, in this passage, Peter is exhorting his readers to remain, to abide, to grow in grace and the knowledge of Jesus the Lord. When one abides, grows in grace and the knowledge of the Lord Jesus, one is not listening to lawless teachers and is not in any danger of falling from one's secure position.

Revelation 3:5—In this verse, Jesus states that He will not blot out the name of those who overcome from the Book of Life. The Book of Life was a listing of all those who are citizens, members of the kingdom of God. It is possible to have one's name erased from the Book of Life (Exodus 32: 32, 33; Psalm 69:18-28). God is the

---

[75]   *Ibid*, 449.

[76]   *Ibid*, 240.

[77]   *Ibid*, 678.

one who will blot the name of a person out of the Book of Life (Exodus 32: 32, 33). Sin is what will cause God to blot a person's name out of His Book (Exodus 32: 33). The act of having one's name blotted, erased from the Book of Life means that one has lost his or her citizenship in God's kingdom (Revelation 20:15). The very fact that it is possible to have one's name blotted from the Book of Life proves that one can reject grace after one has experienced grace.

When we look at the verses that talk of the possibility of apostasy, what we encounter is the fact that the Bible from Genesis to Revelation discusses the concept that apostasy is possible. The teaching of the possibility of apostasy is not found only in one writer but is found throughout the Scriptures.

OBJECTIONS TO THE TEACHING ON THE POSSIBILITY OF APOSTASY

There are objections to the teaching that it is possible for a Christian to commit apostasy. The first objection to the possibility of apostasy is John 10:27-30. In this passage Jesus is describing the unwillingness of some to believe that He was the Messiah. He went on to state that His sheep hear His voice and the fact of someone's unwillingness to listen to Him; this proves that they are not of His sheep. Jesus said that His sheep follow Him. Jesus then states that no one is able to snatch, *harpazo*, His followers out of either His hand or the Father's hand. This word, *harpazo* is also used in 1 Thessalonians 4:17 to describe the future event whereby Christian believers are *snatched or caught up* from this planet and taken to meet the Lord in the air. *harpazo* means to grab or seize by force, with the purpose of removing and/or controlling.[78] To be snatched up or out of the hand of Christ is something that someone or something else does to the Christian. Being snatched out of the hand of God is not something that a Christian can do to his or herself or to other Christians. What this verse is saying is that God is stronger than all else and no one can by force take the followers of Christ. This verse does not however discuss the will of the individual Christian. What we are to understand from this verse is that Jesus is talking about someone else doing the taking of His followers from God. The emphasis is on the other. Jesus in this passage does not say that a saving relationship with Him is a one-way door. Nowhere in this passage does Jesus state that the Christian believer cannot, on his or her own free will, leave the security of the hand of God. There is security in the hand of God and no one can steal or grab a Christian out of the hand of God. The security in the hand of God also eliminates someone forcing a Christian to leave the hand of God involuntarily. However, nowhere

---

[78]   *Ibid,* 221.

in this passage does it say that a Christian cannot choose to voluntarily leave the hand of God.

What Jesus said in John 10: 28 that no one is able to take, snatch, His followers out of either His hand or the Father's hand. In this passage, Jesus is referring to someone else doing the snatching, the taking out of His or the Father's hand. Jesus in this passage has a two-fold purpose. His first purpose was to make clear that the Father is greater than all. His second purpose was to make clear, once again, His one-ness with the Father. He did this to try and convince the Jewish leaders that He, Jesus, was to be followed and not Moses. Another understanding from this passage is of eternal life. Jesus said that He gives to His Followers eternal life and that they will never perish. The Greek construction for never is a double negative, ou me, which indicates an emphatic denial.[79] This objection to the possibility of a Christian committing apostasy is that Christians have been given eternal life. The phrase *eternal life* in many discussions has primarily to do with length of time. Length of time aspect of eternal life, I call the durative element. When duration is the prime meaning of the phrase eternal life, then what must be seen is that all people who have ever lived, are living and will live have eternal life. I am not

---

[79]   H. Dana & J. R. Mantey, *A Manual Grammar of the Greek New Testament*, 266.

referring to what is called universalism. Universalism is the teaching that all people will eventually go to what is called heaven. Universalism is not true. The Bible is clear that all people will not go to heaven. Only the born-again will have a place in heaven. The born-again are those who by faith in Jesus Christ have become righteous (Matthew 25:46). The Bible is also clear that the Non-Christian will be punished forever (Matthew 25:46).

It is this understanding of eternal punishment that falls into the discussion of durative element in the phrase eternal life. We will state an obvious fact and that is if a person will be punished forever, that person must be alive forever. It is not possible to punish a corpse; abuse a corpse, yes. But punish a corpse, no, it is not possible. This means that the people who are punished forever are still living and will live as long as their punishment continues. When Jesus said that there will be those who suffer everlasting, eternal punishment; He also stated that these people will live forever. Thus, we are to understand that the people in Hell, as well as the people in Heaven, will live forever. When the durative element, the length of time perspective of eternal life is the primary understanding; it must be understood that all people no matter where they spend eternity will live forever.

While there is the durative element to eternal life; this, is not the total meaning of what Jesus meant when

He said that He is life (John 14:6) and that He gives life to those who follow Him (John 10:10). When Jesus said that He is life and that He gives life to those who receive Him; He was not simply describing a life lived forever. He was also describing a life that has a certain quality to it. This can be seen in the Greek word for life. The word for life is zoe. zoe means life in its essence.[80] zoe, in addition, when referring to the life Jesus gives to His followers is all the best that Christians have received from God.[81] As the best that Christians have received from God; zoe is a description of Jesus Himself (John 14:6). To understand the meaning of zoe, one has to see the outworking of zoe in the life of Jesus. Jesus does not just live forever. Jesus' life is a life of pure and absolute holiness. Thus, there must be seen the connection between zoe and holiness. Eternal life, thus, is not simply life lived anyway a person wants forever. It is a life that is lived for the purpose of pleasing God in Christ (2 Corinthians 5:9). It is a life of holiness, a life that reflects more and more the character of God Himself. This quality of life only Christians have.

The qualitative element of eternal life, that is holiness, is the primary meaning of the gift of eternal life that Jesus gives to His followers. Jesus gives the Holy Spirit as a gift

---

[80] G. Berry, *A Dictionary of New Testament Greek Synonyms* (Grand Rapids: Zondervan, 1979), 36.

[81] R. Trench, *Synonyms of the New Testament*, 94

to those who follow Him. The Holy Spirit is holy. This is an obvious statement. However, the fact that the Holy Spirit is both holy and the gift of salvation (Ephesians 1:13, 14) which is given to Christians means very clearly that the durative element while true, is not to be understood as the primary element of the gift of eternal life which a Christian receives. As it has been shown above, all people have been given life that will last forever, the durative element. However, not all people have received the gift of the Holy Spirit who is the qualitative element to the gift of eternal life. Because the qualitative element of eternal life is to be seen as the gift given to Christians; the Christian who is not growing in holiness, in Christ-likeness is either back-sliding or is a contradiction, that is not a Christian at all.

There are, thus two aspects to eternal life. The first aspect, for the purpose of understanding the security of the Christian believer is that of quality. The eternal life that Jesus gives to Christians is a life of holiness. The second aspect to the understanding of eternal life is of duration. Jesus has given, by His death and resurrection, eternal life to all people. Jesus, in giving eternal life to every single human being, assures us that no one will ever perish. The identification of eternal life with duration and applying that to only Christian Believers is thus false. Every single human being has been given eternal life. The most important question is where a person will live the eternal life which Jesus has given them.

A second objection to the possibility of a Christian committing apostasy is the claim that if it is possible that a Christian can commit apostasy, then that makes the basis of salvation a basis of works. To answer this objection we turn first of all to the words of Jesus Himself as recorded in John 15:4-6 where Jesus exhorted His followers to remain, abide, meno, in Him. One view of this passage is that Jesus is talking about a fruitful Christian life. This view states that to be fruitful for Christ and the Kingdom of God, one has to abide in Him. While that meaning is partly found in John 15:4. The meaning of this passage is not only a fruitful Christian life but of remaining in Christ Himself. We begin our investigation with the definition of *meno*. *meno* has the meaning of to continue to exist, to remain.[82] The view that states that this passage is referring to only a fruitful Christian and not the possibility of apostasy claim make the claim that a Christian can have a totally fruitless life and remain in Christ, that is continue to be a Christian. However, when we look at the passage again, we discover that Jesus, while discussing a fruitful Christian life also stated that the totally fruitless branch will be cut off by the Father (John 15:2) and thrown into

---

[82]   J. Louw & E. Nida, *Greek-English Lexicon of the New Testament,* 159.

the fire, *kaio,* to be burnt (John 15:6). The fire is not simply referring to the Day of Judgment for Christians. *kaio* is used in 2 Peter 3:12 to describe the destruction of heavens at the Day of God. *kaio* is also used in Hebrews 6:8 to describe land that does not produce fruit; that this land is a cursed land which has no value and in the end will be burnt up. The fire mentioned by Jesus is not simply the fire of the Christian's Judgment, but refers to the fire of destruction. Another reason to understand that this passage is referring to both a fruitful Christian life and the possibility of apostasy is the exhortation by Jesus to remain in Him. That the fruitful branch, the fruitful Christian is the one that abides, remains, continues to exist in Him and has no worry of being cut off by the Father and cast into the fire. If it were not possible for a Christian to leave Christ, which is the opposite of remaining in Him, Jesus would not have exhorted His followers to abide, to remain in Him. This passage is indeed referring to a fruitful Christian life and the need to continue to exist, to abide, to remain in Christ. A third reason to understand that this passage is referring to both a fruitful Christian life and the possibility of apostasy is the fact that the fruitless branch at one time was in Christ but has been cut off of Christ and cast into the fire. This reference is not to the visible Christian organization. This is seen in two reasons: One is the fact that the fruitless branch was in Christ. Jesus said that He is the vine and that the branches were to remain in Him. The second reason is that the visible Christian Church may or may not be in Christ. So, this passage is not referring to those who profess the Christian faith at one time but end up leaving a Christian Church. The fruitless branches that are cut off by the Father and cast into the fire of destruction were at one time *in Christ.*

Jesus goes on to exhort His followers to remain in His love (John 15:9). Love is not to be understood as the warm, fuzzy feeling that is often associated with love. The love that Jesus exhorts His followers to remain in is God Himself; for God is love (1 John 4:16). Jesus is thus exhorting His followers to remain in Him. Jesus is not exhorting His followers to always have the warm fuzzy feeling called love. Another point must be made concerning this exhortation and that is if it were not possible to leave Christ's love, this word of caution would make no sense at all. If the possibility of leaving Christ's love were not possible; why would Jesus exhort His followers to not do the impossible? This exhortation and the many others we have looked at in the New Testament exhorting Christians to not leave grace, to not leave Christ's love, to not fall from grace make no sense at all if it were not possible to commit apostasy, that is to leave grace. In fact, not only do these many exhortations make no sense at all, these exhortations should never have been included in the Word of God in the first place. The reason for this is because the Word of God is the authoritative word to the followers of Christ. A further statement is to be made concerning the people who made these exhortations. If it were not possible for a Christian to leave God's grace and no longer be included in the People of God, the ones who made these exhortations should not be listened to for not only did they not speak the truth, but they flat out lied.

Does the possibility of apostasy mean that salvation and remaining in Christ based on works? The words of Jesus Himself as stated previously answers this question in the negative. To further state a no to this question is the understanding of the relationship of faith and works. Faith is not merely the mental holding to certain Christian truths. The mental holding to Christian truth without the outworking in an ever-increasing holy life means that the so-called faith is dead (James 2:26). Faith is the working out in daily life of Christian truth (James 2:14-26). We see this same truth in Paul when he said that what matters is faith expressing itself in love (Galatians 5:6).

The idea of works also points towards a negative answer to the question of: If there is a possibility of apostasy does that mean salvation is based on works? As has been stated previously, the Law was never given as a means of acceptance with God. What the previous statement means is that a person cannot perform good works so that God accepts him or her in a relationship of righteousness. The fundamental idea behind performing works to gain acceptance with God is flawed and wrong. God cannot be bought off. Acceptance with God is a gift that is offered in Jesus Christ. However, when one accepts the gift of righteousness through Jesus Christ, this does not mean that a righteous relationship with God is not expressed through loving acts towards others. The faith that saves is expressed in works. This is seen by Paul when he stated that by grace are we saved through faith and not through works (Ephesians 2:8, 9). However, Paul does not end there. He goes on to state that salvation, that grace, that faith is expressed in good works (Ephesians 2:10). Does the possibility of apostasy mean that salvation is based on works? The answer is no. However, the truth must be maintained that true faith results in loving acts done to, with and for others. Without these loving acts, what is called faith is dead. Without these good works, true faith, saving faith does not exist.

We return to the original question of this chapter: Can a Christian lose his or her salvation? The phrase *to lose one's salvation* is an unfortunate phrase. We can understand the unfortunate use of lose in reference to salvation by looking at an example. A sports team takes the field with the intention of winning the game. However, at times that sports team will leave the field after losing the game. Their purpose was not to lose but to win. The idea behind to lose is the idea of trying to win but being beaten by the other team. The outcome of the game was just the opposite of what the losing sports team had as its purpose when it first started the game. To lose is to have something go against what is wanted. To lose means something has happened to me that I do not want to happen. When a Christian's heart, will is set on pleasing Christ, this Christian cannot *lose* his or her salvation. The reason being is that to lose means that something has happened to me that I do not want to happen. When I want to please Christ in all things, my will, my heart is fixed on Him. A Christian can, however, after a period of time, if not careful, begin to lose his or her interest in pleasing Christ. When this begins to happen, other objects, goal, purposes take residence in the heart, the will and Christ is slowly crowded into a corner of the heart until there is no more room for Him. When a Christian gets to the place where he or she has lost interest in Christ, the next step is to reject Christ as Lord all together. When a Christian is no longer following Christ as Lord is when the Christian has rejected the once accepted grace of God. When a Christian is no longer following Christ as Lord, this Christian has become fruitless to the point of being cut off by the Father and will eventually be cast into the fire of destruction.

The act of apostasy can be narrowed down to the point where a Christian no longer desires to be obedient to Christ as Lord. This Christian/person has other lords that he/she following. This is the meaning behind Adam and Eve's choice to eat the fruit of the Tree of the Knowledge of Good and Evil. When Adam and Eve chose to listen to the voice of the Serpent and to their own desires, they rejected the Word of God which He had spoken to them and they no longer were obedient to God. When Adam and Eve chose to listen to the voice of the Serpent and to their own desires, God was no longer their Lord; He was no longer the one that they were following. Their hearts were set on other lords, other interests. The result of this choice was that they lost Paradise and they no longer had that intimate relationship with God which the New Testament terms salvation.

Adam and Eve, after they were kicked out of the Garden of Eden; after they lost Paradise; after they lost their relationship with God; did not begin a life of unbridled and uncontrolled sin. They still lived ethical lives. In fact they may have lived lives that are more ethical than many people today, including many Christians.[83] We are thus lead to the understanding that to commit apostasy is found in the will of the human heart. Again we state that a Christian cannot sin his or her way out of grace; a Christian must choose something else as Lord in his or her life. When Christ is no longer Lord, this Christian is no longer obedient to God's Word and thus has lost Paradise, has lost his or her relationship with God.

When it was stated above that a Christian cannot sin his or her way out of grace, what is meant by sin is forgivable sin. The Bible tells us that there is an unforgivable sin, which is in essence to reject Christ as Lord. There are also sins which can be forgiven. The difference between the unforgivable sin and sins which can be forgiven is the attitude of the heart. The unforgivable sin is unforgivable primarily because the Christian refuses to repent. As long as the Christian has the heart to repent when he or she is convicted by the Holy Spirit that Christian has not committed the unforgivable sin. When the Christian, even after the Holy Spirit's conviction, is unwilling to repent and turns his or her heart away from Christ, this Christian is bordering on apostasy.

---

[83] This is found in the manuscript entitled: *The Books of Adam and Eve,* which can be found in the book edited by R.H. Charles: *The Apocrypha and Pseudepigrapha of the Old Testament, Vol. 2* (Berkeley: The Apocryphile Press, 2004), 134-154,

A Christian cannot sin his or her way out of grace. What this means is that a Christian does not have a set number of sins before grace is rejected. Nor is every sin a rejecting of grace. Now, I am certainly not referring to a life lived outside of the moral teachings of Christ. If a person's life is not becoming more and more Christ-like; then there is a real concern of whether that person has truly been born-again. I am certainly not trying to state that as Christians we can live either sinful lives or sinless lives. We will live lives that are far from sinless. However, what is crucial is the will, the desire of the heart. The Christian who is secure in Christ is the one who nourishes the desire to please Christ in all things (2 Corinthians 5:9). The Christian who, while desiring to please Christ in all things, yet, at times stumbles and sins, and then confesses that sin is not in danger of apostasy. The Christian that is in trouble is the one who is losing interest in Christ and faithful living. This Christian is back-sliding; that is heading away from Christ. It is possible for a back-sliding Christian to repent and remain in Christ. There is also the possibility, however, of a back-sliding Christian getting to the point of the unforgivable sin, which is rejecting Christ and turning away from Him. In the words of the writer to the Hebrews, this Christian is deliberately sinning (Hebrews 10:26-29) and is both headed towards and in danger of apostasy.

Because faith is correct Christian doctrine expressed in a life of love and service to God and neighbor; it is possible to stop the holding of correct Christian doctrine and simply live a life of service to others. This life is seen in those who work for the acceptance of certain behaviors that are clearly taught in the Bible as wrong or the view that one birth is enough and people do not need to be born-again. When a Christian does this, this Christian is wandering from the faith. Likewise, it is possible to not live a life of service to God and neighbor while holding to correct Christian doctrine. This life is seen in a life that is active in a Christian fellowship, in singing, in praying; etc., yet, there is no concern for the lost, for the poor, for the widow, for the naked, for the hungry. This life holds tightly to the view that *Jesus loves **me***, but does not hold as passionately the view that Jesus loves you. This life is seen in the concern that God's blessings are to at least maintain my lifestyle if not to improve it. This Christian, while holding to correct Christian doctrines with active involvement in a Christian fellowship has wandered from the faith.

God gives eternal life to His followers many proclaim. Yes, that is true. However, God give eternal life to all people. The only way to understand the truth that there will be some who experience eternal punishment is to come to the conclusion that these people will live forever, that is will live eternally. The only way to live forever is to have eternal life. There is also the proclamation that God's covenants, His promises are eternal. Again, this is true. Yet, we are clearly told in Scripture that it is possible to break God's eternal covenants; His promises (Isaiah 24:5).

When all the previous passages of Scripture are looked at and the teachings combined, one is left with the fact that the possibility of apostasy is clearly taught in the Word of God. Apostasy is to be understood as not sinning one's way out of grace but as the clear, intentional purposeful, rejection of Jesus Christ and His grace. It must be understood that salvation is not a door that once one goes through is *locked* and can never be opened; but salvation is a relationship of love which can be broken at any time.

The Scriptural teaching on human responsibility to choose life over death and the teaching concerning apostasy, adds to the understanding that predestination/election is not individualistic. People, Christians included, can accept and then reject grace, the Lord Jesus and in that acceptance and/or rejection their destinies are then determined.

In the next chapter we will continue to look at the destinies of individuals in light of whether or not God's decrees are fixed or whether there is room in the decrees of God for individual destinies to change.

CHAPTER 3

GOD'S DECREES ARE NOT FIXED (CLOSED)

In the previous two chapters, it has been stated that election/predestination is corporate and not individualistic. To support that statement, in the last chapter, the Scriptural teaching on apostasy was examined. In that examination it was found that the Word of God teaches that it is possible for a person to become a Christian and for that very same Christian, while in grace, to reject that grace and to once again be counted within the number of those heading for hell.

In this chapter the decrees of God will be looked at to determine whether God's decrees are fixed or not. By the use of the term fixed is meant that once God decrees something, then that is a fixed result; nothing can alter that choice of God or the resultant consequences that come out of that decree. If the decrees of God are fixed, then individuals do not have a choice; their destinies are set even before they are born. If however, God's decrees are not fixed but there is room within the decrees for human choice, then this will aid in our understanding that election/predestination is corporate and not individualistic.

We begin with the statement that if the decrees of God are fixed, then there is a huge discrepancy with the teaching on apostasy. It has been shown in the previous chapter that there is ample evidence within the Scriptural record itself to come to the conclusion that the possibility of apostasy is taught. If God's decrees are fixed, there is then a contradiction within the Word of God itself.

Are God's decrees fixed or is there room within them for human responsibility? To answer this question we look at Romans 9:21 and the image of the potter and the clay. Barth says that the image of the potter and the clay points to the proper understanding of creation.[84] Osborne says that the image of the potter and the clay states that the Creator controls his creation and has the sovereign right to form whatever he wishes in his created order.[85] Cranfield states that the image of the potter and the clay brings out that God has ultimate authority to appoint individuals to various functions within His over-all purpose.[86]

The image of the potter and the clay is used in various passages other than Romans 9:21. It is to these other passages that we turn in order to understand what Paul meant by his use of the potter and clay imagery.

---

[84]   Karl Barth, trans. By Edwyn Hoskins, *The Epistle to the Romans* (London: Oxford University Press, 1968), 357.

[85]   Osborne, *Romans*, 252.

[86]   Cranfield, *The International Critical Commentary on Romans, Vol. Vol. 2,* 492.

Isaiah 29:16 and Isaiah 45:9 both use the image of the potter and the clay and state the total futility of the creature to criticize the creator.

Isaiah 64:8 reflects the true relationship between the creation and the creator. This relationship is to be seen as God is the father of creation.

Jeremiah 18:5-10 is perhaps one of the main passages that helps explain and make clear the meaning of Paul in Romans 9:20, 21. For that reason we will spend more time on this passage in order to understand the meaning of the potter and the clay.

In Jeremiah 18: 5-10 God asks Israel if He cannot do with her as the potter does with the clay (Jeremiah 18:5, 6). Here again is the right of the creator to do as He wishes with the creation. After God restated to Israel that He, God has the right to do with Israel and in that sense with all other nations; God makes clear a very fundamental issue in the understanding of the potter and clay imagery and in the discussion of whether God's decrees are fixed.

God, by the use of four *ifs*, makes clear an essential issue in the relationship between God and His creation.

1. If at any time, God says, that I announce that a nation or kingdom is to be uprooted . . .

2. If that nation I warned repents of its evil, then I will relent and not inflict on it the disaster that I had planned.

3. If at another time I announce that a nation or kingdom is to be built up and planted . . .

4. If that nation does evil in my sight and does not obey me, then I will reconsider the good I had intended to do for it.

There are in Jeremiah 18:5-10 two decrees of God. These decrees are found in the words *planned* and *intended.* There is also to be found within this passage human responsibility. Human responsibility is found within the second and fourth *if statement.* What Jeremiah 18: 5-10 teaches is that if, after God has decreed a certain course of action, a certain destiny if you will, for a particular nation, and that nation repents from its evil or obedience, then God will change his plan/intention for that nation or kingdom.

The unrighteous nation or people have, so to speak, God's judgment residing on them (See Romans 1:18 where Paul wrote that the wrath of God is being revealed on all forms of wickedness). If that nation which is under the judgment/wrath of God, repents; then God will *relent* and change His plan for that nation (Jeremiah 18:8). The words in the NIV *relent* (Jeremiah 18:8) and *reconsider*

(Jeremiah 18:10) are both from the same Hebrew word (naham). Naham tells us that from God's perspective, prophecy and judgment is conditioned upon the response of people.[87] The Septuagint, in Jeremiah 18: 8, 10 for naham uses metanoeo. Metanoeo means: to repent, to change purpose not yet executed, to reconsider.[88] Metanoeo is the same verb used in Jonah 3:9 where it is stated that God may yet *relent* and with compassion turn from his fierce anger. The word *turn* means to turn back, to turn away, to turn away from, to change the fortune of, to avert.[89] The Septuagint uses a double negative in Jonah 3:9 where it is translated *so that we will not perish.* The use in the Greek of a double negative indicates an emphatic denial.[90] Thus, if God relents and turns with compassion from His fierce anger, we will in no way perish. In Jonah 3:10 it is stated that this is what happened. God saw that the people turned from their evil way and He repented (Septuagint) from the evil which he had threatened.

---

[87]   R. Laird Harris, ed., *Theological Wordbook of the Old Testament, Vol. 2* (Chicago: Moody Press, 1981), 571.

[88]   J. Lust, *A Greek-English Lexicon of the Septuagint, Part 2* (Stuttgart: Deutsche Bibelgesellschaft, 1996), 300.

[89]   J. Lust, *A Greek-English Lexicon of the Septuagint, Part I* (Stuttgart: Deutsche Bibelgesellschaft, 1992), 56.

[90]   H. Dana & J. R. Mantey, *A Manual Grammar of the Greek New Testament*, 266.

When God saw that the people turned from their evil way, He did not bring upon them the destruction that He had threatened (NIV). The Hebrew word translated *threatened* is davar. Davar means to speak and is used of divine utterances.[91] It is used in 2 Samuel 23:2 to describe the Spirit of the Lord speaking through David. Davar is used to describe the Word of God (1 Chronicles 17:3). The word davar tells us that when God threatened (davar) to bring destruction upon the people; it was God's intention to do so. In other words, the use of davar tells us that God had every intention of destroying the people. God's davar is not empty or void but will accomplish what God desires and His purpose for which it proceeded from His mouth (Isaiah 55:11). The people of Nineveh were faced with the real, intended Word of God that He would actually destroy them.

The people of Nineveh, facing the real threat of destruction, repented and turned from their evil way. God, upon seeing their repentance, changed His intention for them. What is to be seen is that a change in the heart of a man or woman will result in a change in God's judgment; God's plan for that individual. God's action is predicated on human action; there is within the decrees of God *room* for human responsibility.

---

[91]   Girdlestone, *Synonyms of the Old Testament,* 205.

It is also to be seen that God's decrees do not determine human responsibility. This is seen also in Exodus 32:9-14.

In Exodus 32: 9-14 God intends to destroy his people which He brought out of slavery in Egypt (Exodus 32: 10). Moses, acting as the mediator for these people, appeals to God's favor to not destroy this people. In this case it is stated that God relented from His plan/intention to destroy them.

2 Chronicles 12:1-7 tells of the time when Rehoboam became king in Israel. After Rehoboam had established himself as king, we are told that he and all Israel with him abandoned the Lord (2 Chronicles 12: 1). The consequence of Rehoboam and Israel's decision to abandon the Lord was that their enemy, Shishak, king of Egypt attacked Israel and began to capture the cities of Judah and approached Jerusalem itself. At that time, the prophet Shemaiah approached Rehoboam and the leaders of Judah and said to them: This is what the Lord says, 'You have abandoned me; therefore, I abandon you to Shishak' (2 Chronicles12: 5).

You have abandoned me; therefore I abandon you . . .in the Hebrew the word used in both phrases is the same. This word azab means to leave, forsake.[92] The meaning then is since Rehoboam and all Israel had forsaken the

---

[92]   R. Laird Harris, *Theological Wordbook of the Old Testament, Vol. 2*, 658.

Lord; the Lord was going to do the same that is to forsake them to Sishak king of Egypt.

However, as the prophet Shemaiah spoke these words to Rehoboam and to the leaders, they humbled themselves and said that the Lord is just (2 Chronicles 12: 6). At this point, when the Lord had seen that Rehoboam and the leaders had humbled themselves; the Lord changed His plan for them and said that they would not be abandoned; not destroyed by Sishak, king of Egypt (2 Chronicles 12: 7).

The Lord changed His plan, His intention for Rehoboam as well as for Israel. We are told that because Rehoboam had humbled himself, the Lord's anger turned from him and Rehoboam was not destroyed (2 Chronicles 12:12).

Exodus 4:24-26 states that God had the intention of killing Moses. The reason that God intended to kill Moses seems to be that he had failed to circumcise his son. We see this explained by the actions of Zipporah, Moses wife, who took a knife and circumcised their son. Because Zipporah had done this, God did not kill Moses, but left him alone. What is taught is that because Zipporah, Moses' wife, acted for him, God then changed his mind and let Moses live

Joel 2:13 teaches that when people return to the Lord, the Lord will relent from sending calamity. The word *relent* is Nacham. Nacham, when used in reference to

God, means there is implied an idea of change and perhaps of sorrow, but not the consciousness of wrongdoing.[93] The idea of God relenting or changing His intention for a people is stated again in Psalm 106: 40-45 and in Amos 7: 1-6.

The decrees of God set boundaries for the creation to function within. However, God's decrees are not so fixed as to determine what choice an individual will make. To understand this statement, we will look at the Scriptural teaching on the influence through grace and the Holy Spirit that God accompanies His decrees.

God does not simply give decrees and leave humanity to find their own way. God sends His Spirit to aid the human individual in the choice that is to be made. This is seen in the description of Jesus as the true light (John 1: 9). As the true light, Jesus gives light to every man (John 1:9). The phrase *every man* is from the Greek *pas anthropos*. Pas means the totality of any objective, mass, collective.[94] Anthropos means human being.[95] Thus, *pas anthropos* means the totality of the human race.

---

[93]   R. Girdlestone, *Synonyms of the Old Testament*, 89.

[94]   Louw & Nida, *Greek-English Lexicon of the New Testament*, 597.

[95]   *Ibid*, 104.

Jesus, the true light, has given light to every human being. This is done by means of the conscience[96] and by means of the Holy Spirit who convicts the world[97] in regard to sin and righteousness and judgment (John 16:8-11). The conviction of the world by the Holy Spirit in regard to sin is because the whole world does not believe in Jesus (John 16:9). The conviction by the Holy Spirit in regard to righteousness because Jesus is going to the Father; and finally, the conviction in regard to judgment because the Prince of this world now stands condemned (John 16:10, 11).

What is to be understood from the words of Jesus is that the whole world stands accountable to God for his or her belief/lack of belief in Jesus. The belief or lack of belief in Jesus results in righteousness or the lack of righteousness and damnation or the lack of damnation in the Day of Judgment. The *whole world* is under the conviction of the Holy Spirit for their belief or lack of belief in Jesus. The fact that the whole world is under the conviction of the Holy Spirit means that the whole world is accountable for their lack of belief or belief.

---

[96] J. Wesley on John 1:9 in his *Notes on the News Testament* (Kansas City: Beacon Hill Press, 1983).

[97] World is kosmos which means the entire universe and everything in it (Louw & Nida, *Greek-English Lexicon,* 1).

What is to be understood from the teaching Christ enlightening everyone and that the whole world is accountable for his or her belief or lack of is the fact that within creation and with the presence of the Holy Spirit, there is enough for people to turn to God.

Paul says the same thing twice in Romans. The first time is in Romans 1: 18-32. In this passage Paul states that what may be known about God is plain to everyone, even the ones who reject this evidence (Romans 1:18-19). The evidence that is plain to the world is sufficient to remove any excuse to not believe (Romans 1: 20). Paul goes on to say that although the world knows that God exists (Romans 1:21); they did not glorify Him nor were they thankful to Him (Romans 1: 21). In fact, instead of glorifying God; the world exchanged the glory of God for images (Romans 1: 23). Because the world rejected God and began to worship images, God gave them over to sexual impurity (Romans 1: 24). While in the midst of sexual impurity; the world exchanged the truth of God for a lie and worshipped and served created things (Romans 1: 25). Because the world worshipped and served created things; God gave them over to shameful lusts (Romans 1: 26). While the world was indulging shameful lusts; they even rejected the knowledge of God altogether (Romans 1: 28). Because the world rejected the knowledge of God; God gave them over to a depraved mind (Romans 1: 28).

In summary, Paul states that although the world knew God's righteous standards; they not only continued to practice unrighteousness but also to approve those who practice them (Romans 1: 32).

Within Romans 1: 18-32 the phrase *God gave them over* three times (Romans 1: 24, 26, 28). This phrase and the causative actions of the world describe how God relates to the world. We begin with the phrase itself. Osborne says that this phrase means that God handed them over to the results of their sin.[98] Cranfield says that the phrase in question must be understood in *terms of permitting, in the sense not of authorizing but of not preventing, of withholding His help which alone could prevent.*[99] There is a caution that must be sounded here. This caution is the understanding that in the action of God giving them up, there is a sense of finality. The same Greek word translated *gave up* used in Romans 1:24, 26, 28 is also used in Romans 8: 32 where it is stated that God gave up His son to death for us all. Yet, in no way is it understood that Jesus was delivered over to death forever.

Cranfield's understanding of this phrase is enlightening. He says:

---

[98] Osborne, *Romans*, 51.

[99] CEB Cranfield, *The International Critical Commentary on Romans, Vol. 2*, 121.

> *We must understand this phrase to mean*
> *that God allowed them to go their own way*
> *in order that they might at last learn from*
> *their consequent wretchedness to hate the*
> *futility of a life turned away from the truth*
> *of God. We suggest then that Paul's meaning*
> *is neither that these fell out of the hands of*
> *God, nor that God washed His hands of them,*
> *but rather that this delivering them up was*
> *a deliberate act of judgment and mercy on*
> *the part of God who smites in order to heal*
> *(Isaiah 19:22) and that throughout the time of*
> *their God-forsakenness God is still concerned*
> *with them and dealing with them.*[100]

In the meaning of the phrase, *God gave them* up, Paul alludes to Romans 2:4 where he stated that God's patience leads to repentance. The ideas of God's patience leading to repentance is found also in 2 Peter 3:9 where it is clearly stated that God does not want anyone to perish but for everyone to come to repentance.

There is a process set forth in Romans 1: 18-32. This process states that when people reject the evidence of God around them, the voice of their conscience and the conviction of the Holy Spirit, and they begin to worship

---

[100]   Cranfield, *Vol. 1,* 121.

and serve things other than God; God removes His hand and they receive the consequences of their own actions. We must state clearly that God does not cause them to reject Him. God's actions were in response to the actions of the world itself. This relationship between God and the world is expressed clearly by Paul when he states that the rejection of Israel was due to their rejection of Christ (Romans 9:30-33).

The relationship between God and the world as expressed and found in God's intentions/decrees and the room within these decrees is difficult to understand. On the one hand, God' choice does not depend on humans (Romans 9:16-18). On the other hand, however, Israel's rejection was because of her unbelief Romans 9:30-32. We are to further understand that God is not arbitrary in His dealings with the world. Romans 9:18 cannot mean that God is arbitrary in his mercy, because Israel's rejection is based on her unbelief (Rom 9:30-32). There is to be found in these two poles these truths: that God shows mercy on those who turn to him in faith and hardens those who refuse to do so and that God at times limits His sovereignty to give room for human response. If there is no room within the intentions of God for response, how did Satan fall? How did Adam and Eve fall from grace. If there is no room within God's intentions then Satan must have been created evil and Adam and Eve were created sinful.

The teaching that within the intentions of God is room for human response and repentance is found also in Acts 3:17-23. In this passage Peter, speaking to those gathered at Solomon's Colonnade said that God prophesied that Christ would suffer by the hands of mankind. Peter goes on to say that those who did this acted in ignorance. Peter emphasizes that those who acted according to God's plan were also included within the scope of Christ's death and God's love, as Jesus was appointed even for the ones who acted in ignorance (v. 20). What this means is that the plan of God for Christ to suffer did not condemn those who killed Him for all eternity; there was still opportunity for them to repent.

The decrees of God have room for human response. This is seen also in 2 Corinthians 5: 11-21. In this passage, Paul wrote that God has reconciled the world to Himself (v. 19) and now is pleading through Paul for the world to be reconciled to God (v. 20, 21). God has done a universal work in Christ, which is to reconcile the world to Himself. Now, God has created *room* within His work for the world to either accept or reject this reconciliation. If God's decrees/plans were fixed, that is closed and there was no room for human response, why then would God plead through Paul or anyone else for the world to be reconciled? A closed decree by God would mean that there would be no need for God to plead for the world's response. The fact that God is pleading for the world to accept reconciliation and become reconciled to God means that there is room within the decree, the work of God for human response.

CHAPTER 4

HARDENING OF THE HEART

There is found within the decrees of God, *room* for human response. What is meant by this is that God has not decreed with the understanding of causation everything to happen. The opposite idea is that God from eternity past made the decision of who would be saved and who would be remain in sin. Found within this understanding is the teaching that once God decreed/decided who would be saved and who would remain in sin; the individuals affected by the choice of God had no recourse, no room to decide anything on his or her own. The decision of God in affect was the decision that determined each individual's destiny. God picked the individuals who would believe and, depending upon whether the view held, God either left the remaining individuals in sin or picked/chose them for eternal damnation.[101]

---

[101]   There is found within what is called Calvinism two views. One is called single predestination which teaches that God chose those who would believe out of the mass of humanity heading for damnation. The second is called double predestination which teaches that God not only picked/chose those who would believe but also chose/picked those who would spend eternity in hell.

The previous chapters has shown that there is enough evidence to question whether either one of these views is correct. The Scriptural evidence discussed includes: the use of the individual to represent the whole; the divine command/exhortation to choose life over death; the ability of apostasy; Christ as the Lamb of God who died for the sins of the whole world, which includes every single human being; and the process whereby God *gives up* individuals to the result of his or her own choice.

In this chapter, Romans 9:17, 18—the hardening of Pharaoh's heart will be discussed. The purpose of this discussion is to come to the understanding of who hardened Pharaoh's heart and the relationship between God and Pharaoh, who could represent every person.

We begin our discussion in the book of Exodus where the account of God's relationship with Pharaoh is described. What is discovered when Exodus is studied is that the hardening of Pharaoh's heart is mentioned 18 times. In 9 of those 18 times the hardening of Pharaoh's heart is ascribed to God (7:3; 9:12; 10:1, 20, 27: 11:10; 14:4, 8) and in 9 of those 18 times Pharaoh is said to have hardened his own heart (7:13-14, 22; 8:15, 19, 32; 9:7, 34-35).

The times when Pharaoh hardened his own heart are after the first five plagues:

1. Plague of blood—Exodus 7:13-14, 22
2. Plague of frogs—Exodus 8:15
3. Plague of gnats—Exodus 8:19
4. Plague of flies—Exodus 8:32
5. Plague on livestock—Exodus 9:7

It was after the fifth plague and at the sixth plague is stated that God hardened pharaoh's heart (Exodus 9:12).

6. Plague of boils—Exodus 9:12
7. Plague of hail—Exodus 9:34, 34
8. Plague of locusts—Exodus 10:1, 20
9. Plague of darkness—Exodus 10:27
10. Plague on firstborn—Exodus 11

When the plagues are looked at, it will be seen that the first nine plagues can be divided into three groups of three plagues each. These groups are:

1. Exodus 7:14-8:19
2. Exodus 8:20-9:12
3. Exodus 9:13-10:29

What is important in the grouping of these plagues is that with the first plague in each group (the first, fourth and seventh) the plague was introduced by a warning delivered to Pharaoh in the morning. For the first three plagues the warning to Pharaoh is found in Exodus7:15-18. The warning to Pharaoh for the second group of three plagues is Exodus 8: 20-21. The final warning given to Pharaoh by God heading up the final group of three plagues is Exodus 9:13-14.

When the total picture of the hardening of Pharaoh's heart is examined; what will be discovered is that Pharaoh alone was the one who hardened his own heart in each of the first five plagues. It was not until the sixth plague is it stated that God hardened the heart of Pharaoh. The conclusion then is that in the sixth plague, after Pharaoh's continued refusal to obey the Word of God; did God confirm Pharaoh's willful action as God told Moses that he would do so (Exodus 4:21).

The process seen in the interaction of God and Pharaoh was described by Paul in Romans 1: 18-32. We repeat from the previous chapter our discussion on Romans 1:18-32 so that the process described by Paul can be seen at work in the life of Pharaoh. In Romans 1: 18-32 Paul states that what may be known about God is plain to everyone, even the ones who reject this evidence (Romans 1:18-19). The evidence that is plain to the world is sufficient to remove any excuse to not believe (Romans 1: 20). Paul goes on to say that although the world knows that God exists (Romans 1:21); they did not glorify Him nor were they thankful to Him (Romans 1: 21). In fact, instead of glorifying God; the world exchanged the glory of God for images (Romans 1: 23). Because the world rejected God and began to worship images, God gave them over to sexual impurity (Romans 1: 24). While in the midst of sexual impurity; the world exchanged the truth of God for a lie and worshipped and served created things (Romans 1: 25). Because the world worshipped and served created things; God gave them over to shameful lusts (Romans 1: 26). While the world was indulging shameful lusts; they even rejected the knowledge of God altogether (Romans 1: 28). Because the world rejected the knowledge of God; God gave them over to a depraved mind (Romans 1: 28). In summary, Paul states that although the world knew God's righteous standards; they not only continued to practice unrighteousness but also to approve those who practice them (Romans 1: 32).

Within Romans 1: 18-32 the phrase *God gave them over* three times (Romans 1: 24, 26, 28). This phrase and the causative actions of the world describe how God relates to the world. We begin with the phrase itself. Osborne says that this phrase means that God handed them over to the results of their sin.[102] Cranfield says that the phrase in question must be understood in *terms of permitting, in the sense not of authorizing but of not preventing, of*

---

[102] Osborne, *Romans*, 51.

withholding His help which alone could prevent.[103] There is a caution that must be sounded here. This caution is the understanding that in the action of God giving them up, there is a sense of finality. The same Greek word translated *gave up* used in Romans 1:24, 26, 28 is also used in Romans 8: 32 where it is stated that God gave up His son to death for us all. Yet, in no way is it understood that Jesus was delivered over to death forever.

There is a process set forth in Romans 1: 18-32. This process states that when people reject the evidence of God around them, the voice of their conscience and the conviction of the Holy Spirit, and they begin to worship and serve things other than God; God removes His hand and they receive the consequences of their own actions. We must state clearly that God does not cause them to reject Him. God's actions were in response to the actions of the world itself. This relationship between God and the world is expressed clearly by Paul when he states that the rejection of Israel was due to their rejection of Christ (Romans 9:30-33).

The truth found in the discussion regarding the hardening of Pharaoh's heart is that God hardened an already unrepentant, stubborn, callous heart. God did not harden a heart open to Him. The hardening of the heart is

---

[103]   CEB Cranfield, *The International Critical Commentary on Romans, Vol. I,* 121.

described in Scripture as the both the decision of Pharaoh and as the work of God. Girdlestone sees in the discussion concerning the hardening of Pharaoh's heart a universal principle. He states:

> *Pharaoh's case is by no means unique; it is a sample of the history of all those who neglect the opportunities which God gives them, and thus lead Him to put in exercise that law to which the whole human race is subject—that moral impressions, if not acted upon, become (subjectively) weaker and weaker until finally the heart of man becomes altogether callous.*[104]

The understanding that the hardening of Pharaoh's heart is a universal principle is also taught by Paul in Romans 1: 18-32. In the discussion of hardening of Pharaoh's heart is found the principle that God confirmed/ gave Pharaoh over the consequences of his own decision. It is vital to the meaning of Paul in Romans 9: 17, 18 in his discussion of the hardening of Pharaoh's heart to locate that discussion within the context of the epistle to the Romans up to the point in question. To simply take the discussion of the hardening of Pharaoh's heart out

---

[104]   Girdlestone, *Synonyms of the Old Testament,* 66.

of the total context of both Romans and the teaching of Scripture is to do an injustice to the text and to what God is conveying to the world.

The discussion of the hardening of Pharaoh's heart is found within the immediate context of Paul's use of the imagery of the potter and the clay (Romans 9:17-24). The imagery of the potter and the clay has already been discussed, see chapter 4 of this study. After the many passages where the potter and clay imagery are stated, the full meaning of Romans 9: 17-24 is to be understood. The meaning of Paul's use of the potter and clay imagery cannot be divorced from the meaning of this imagery found throughout the Scriptures. Paul understood that the Gospel and the whole Scriptures were of divine origin. He stated that Scriptures were inspired by God (2 Timothy 3:16).[105] The Scriptures to Paul included the Old Testament as well as the New Testament. As he stated that the Gospel he received was received by a direct revelation, appearance of Jesus Christ (Galatians 1: 11, 12). Because Paul had received the Gospel from Jesus Christ directly; it is to be understood that Paul also understood that Jesus Christ is the fulfillment of the Old Testament (Matthew 5:17). In addition, Paul did not hesitate to connect the teaching of the Gospel with the Old Testament; as is seen in the many instances where Paul

---

[105] The Greek word translated *inspired* literally means God-breathed.

quoted the Old Testament. Since Paul had such a view and use of the Scriptures, it is only natural to understand the meaning of the potter and clay imagery used by Paul as the meaning taught in the whole Scriptures.

When Paul's view of and use of the Scriptures is understood, to understand the meaning behind his use of the potter and clay imagery, Jeremiah 18: 7-10 must be one of the central stands to the meaning Paul was conveying. In other words, Paul did not mean in his use of the potter and clay imagery that God made decisions arbitrarily or that God's decisions/decrees were fixed or closed. Paul intends to convey by his use of the potter and clay imagery that within the decrees/intentions/decisions by God is room for human response and that human beings can change the destiny that is set for them by their acceptance or rejection of God's grace.

We will summarize the discussion of the potter and the clay with a quote from Cranfield who says: *that it cannot be emphasized too strongly that there is naturally not the slightest suggestion that the potter's freedom is the freedom of caprice, and that it is, therefore, perverse to suppose that what Paul wanted to assert was a freedom of the Creator to deal with His creatures according to some indeterminate, capricious, absolute will.*[106]

---

[106] Cranfield, *The International Critical Commentary on Romans, Vol. 2.* 492.

Within the discussion regarding the potter and the clay, Paul states that there are pots/vessels for noble purposes and some for common use (Romans 9:21). The first comment to be made is regarding the stuff from which the pots made for noble purpose and the pots made for common purpose are made. The pottery of noble and common purposes were made of the same stuff, that is from the same lump of clay (Romans 9:21). The difference is not the material or the shape of the pottery/vessel. What makes a vessel holy, or of noble purpose is the fact that it has been made holy by being consecrated to God. In Exodus 30:18 the vessels in the temple were made of bronze, a common material. What made the vessels in the temple holy was that they were dedicated to God (Exodus 30: 26-29).

The second comment regarding the pots is that the description of *common use* implies menial use, not reprobation or destruction. A very insightful comment is made by Cranfield when he says that the potter does not make ordinary, everyday pots, merely in order to destroy them.[107]

At this point, our discussion will focus on the vessels/pots that Paul calls the objects of God's wrath. In the Greek of Romans 9:22, the word *prepared* in the phrase *prepared for destruction* which Paul uses to describe certain pots

---

[107]   *Ibid*, footnote #2, 492.

or vessels, is an accusative plural, neuter, perfect middle/ passive participle. It is a known grammatical principle that a participle will agree with its antecedent, the word that it modifies. The word that *prepared* modifies is *vessels*. What is to be remembered is that the perfect middle/ passive participles share the same form.[108]

Since the participle in Romans 9:22 is a middle/ passive; it is important to understand the distinction between the middle and the passive. The meaning of the Greek passive is that the subject is receiving the action;[109] that is something is done to the subject. The meaning of the middle is that the subject participates in the results of the action;[110] that is the subject does something to itself. A further distinction of the middle voice is that the middle voice emphasizes the agent of the action.[111]

---

[108] J. Gresham Machen, *New Testament Greek for Beginners* (Toronto: Macmillan, 1951), 186; William Chamberlain, *An Exegetical Grammar of the Greek New* Testament (Grand Rapids: Baker Book House, 1979), 97; Ernest Colwell, *A Beginner's Reader for the New Testament Greek* (New York: Harper & Row, 1965), 48.

[109] Dana & Mantey, *A Manual Grammar of the Greek New Testament,* p. 161; Kenneth Wuest, *The Practical Use of the Greek New Testament* (Chicago: Moody Press, 1982), 40.

[110] Dana & Mantey, *A Manual Grammar of the Greek New Testament,* p. 157.

[111] *Ibid,* 157.

The importance of understanding the participle translated *prepared* in Romans 9: 22 is since the perfect middle/passive participles share the same form, the meaning is to be drawn from the context of the letter to the Romans. If the participle *prepared* is middle; then the vessels prepared themselves for destruction. If the participle *prepared* is passive; then the meaning is that God prepared the vessels for destruction.

The discussion of the vessels of wrath continues by Paul when he states that the vessels of wrath are endured by God with great patience (Romans 9: 22). Paul has already mentioned the patience of God in Romans 2:4. In Romans 2:4, the patience of God is said to be that which leads to salvation. God's patience in romans 9:22 and in Romans 2:4 are connected with His kindness and intended to lead those whom He endures to repentance. The expression vessels of wrath indicate that those who are so called are indeed objects of God's wrath *at the time in question.* However this does not mean that they must always remain objects of wrath. This understanding is gained when Romans 9:22 is compared with Ephesians 2:3. In Ephesians 2:3, Paul states that *we like the rest were children of wrath.* Here is the point in question: Paul goes on to say that *we who were children of wrath at one time* are now believers and are no longer children of wrath. We see in Ephesians 2:3 the principle that it is possible, *at one time*, to be children of wrath and *at another time*, because of faith in Christ, to no longer be under God's wrath. This is the same principle that Paul is explaining in Romans 9:22. What we are to understand in the discussion regarding the patience of God is that God's purpose for the vessels of wrath is that they would become vessels of mercy (Romans 9: 22-24). The understanding of the participle translated *prepared* as a middle voice is consistent with what Paul said in Romans 1: 18-32; 9:17; and 9:30-33 where Paul states clearly that the reason that Israel was rejected was that Israel rejected faith righteousness in Christ.

The discussion of the vessels of wrath whether they are eternally vessels of wrath or is there a possibility that they might become vessels of mercy is continued by Paul in Romans 11. Paul asks, because of the teaching of Romans 1-10 and righteousness by faith, if God has rejected His people (Romans 11:1). Paul states that God has not rejected His people whom He foreknew. He bases his answer on three points.

The first point is found in the meaning of the word *foreknew.* This word can mean to know about something prior to some temporal reference point[112] and can also mean to choose in advance.[113] Foreknew refers to the

---

[112] Louw & Nida, *Greek-English Lexicon,* 335.

[113] *Ibid,* 363.

general election of the people of Israel as a whole.[114] In addition, the word, *know* is used in Scripture to designate a personal relationship between two individuals (Genesis 4:1). The meaning of Paul's use of the word *foreknew* is that God has not rejected His people in which God had a personal relationship with.

The second point is Paul himself. Paul is an Israelite and has believed in Jesus Christ Romans 11:2). The third point Paul bases his position on is Scripture. He quotes 1 Kings 19: 10, 14 where Elijah states that *he is the only one who has remained faithful to God.* God's answer to Elijah was that God had reserved for Himself seven thousand who had not bowed the knee to Baal (Romans 11: 2-4). Paul drew from that Old Testament passage the fact that there is a remnant for God (Romans 11:5).

In an effort to understand how this relates to the vessels of wrath and of mercy; we begin with the number seven thousand. The number seven thousand both in Romans 11:4 and in I kings 19: 18 is to be understood as a round number and as an estimate of those who remained faithful. The number seven thousand is to be understood in the light of the meaning attached to the number seven and to multiples of seven in the Bible and in Judaism. Within the Bible and Judaism, the number seven was as

---

[114] Cranfield, *The International Critical Commentary on Romans, Vol. 2,* 545.

a symbol of completeness, perfection.[115] Because seven thousand is to be understood as a round number and as a symbol of completeness; God's statement that He is preserving for Himself seven thousand men in Israel is a declaration of His faithfulness to his purpose of salvation for his people, and indicating that the remnant is not closed but an open number.[116]

The hardening of the heart is not something that is not irreversible. In other words, when the heart is hardened, even by God, there is room within the decrees/intentions/acts of God for human response. When humans respond in faith God will then relate differently to that individual. Paul states this very clearly when he says that the hardening of the heart is not a once-for-all act (Romans 11:7-11).

Paul says that the hardening of the heart of Israel (Romans 11:7) is experienced in their receiving a spirit of stupor, eyes that cannot see and ears that cannot hear (Romans 11:7, 8). This quote used in Isaiah 29: 10 described the condition of prophets and seers and in Deuteronomy 29:4 to describe the condition of the people of Israel is also found with a promise. Although God had caused a deep sleep to fall upon the people, there is the day coming when the deaf will hear and the blind see (Isaiah 29: 18). In other words, although God caused a deep sleep/stupor

---

[115] *Ibid*, 547.
[116] *Ibid*, 548.

to fall upon those who have not believed; this deep sleep/ stupor is not the final condition. There is a time coming when those who sleep can be, if they choose, wakened. This promise Paul extends to Israel when he states that the present condition of Israel is not eternal or permanent, but Israel will awaken to the Gospel message (Romans 11: 25, 26).

The hardening of the heart which resulted in Israel's stumbling and in becoming a stumbling block (Romans 11: 9) is not a permanent condition. He states that the ones whose heart has been hardened, are not destined to stumble, to be hardened forever. He states this by asking the question: *Did they stumble so as to fall beyond recovery?* (Romans 11: 11). The word translated *fall beyond recovery* when used in a religious or moral sense has the meaning of *fall from the state of grace.*[117] The *falling beyond recovery* is in a purpose/result clause.[118] The negative Paul used in this verse denies the result/

---

[117] William Arndt and F. Wilbur Gingrich, *A Greek-English Lexicon of the New Testament and Other Early Christian Literature*, 660.

[118] Chamberlain says that purpose/result clauses are often introduced by the same conjunction and that purpose is simply intended result and result is accomplished purpose (Chamberlain, *An Exegetical Grammar of the Greek New Testament*, 182.

purpose clause as final. In other words, those who stumble have not stumbled to their eternal damnation.[119]

When all of the previous is taken into account, it is to be seen that the hardening of the heart is not necessarily the final condition for the individual. There is room within the decrees of God for human response, for individuals to repent and respond to the Gospel in faith. When those who, at the present time are hardened, repent and believe, God will then change His intention in regards to them (Jeremiah 18: 7-10).

Do we human beings truly have a real choice? Or do we simply choose that which has been chosen/ordained for us to choose? In this section we will look at various Scriptures that refer to the act of choice and the human will.

We begin with words that refer to the human will. First of all there is nadav. This word is used of the freedom of the will and refers to voluntary action and not action that is forced or compulsory.[120] Harris says that nadav means an uncompelled and free movement of the will.[121] A second word for the human will is avah. Avah refers to the inclination which leads to action.[122] When avah

---

[119] Cranfield, *The International Critical Commentary on Romans, Vol. 2,* 555.

[120] Girdlestone, *Synonyms of the Old Testament, 70.*

[121] Harris, *Theological Wordbook of the Old Testament*, 554.

[122] Girdlestone, *Synonyms of the Old Testament*, 67.

refers to the disobedience of Israel, the meaning is that the refusal to obey God's Word was voluntary. [123] The Septuagint translates avah as boulomai and thelo.[124] Thelo and boulomai are used in the New Testament to express willingness, desire and wish.[125]

The free movement of the will is found in the teaching that God changes his mind/plan for individuals and nations based on the human response (Exodus 32:11-14; Jeremiah 18:5-10; Jeremiah 18:11, 12; 2 Chronicles 12:5-7, 12; 2 Chronicles 7:4). The teaching that there is a free movement of the will is found also in the fact that Jesus not only fulfilled the Old Testament but is also the embodiment of its teaching (Matthew 5:17). The teaching of a free movement of the will which was first revealed in the Old Testament era is carried over into the New Testament era.

The free choice of humans is also found in Romans 1:28. Paul wrote that the wicked did not think that it was worthwhile to retain the knowledge of God. Osborne states that what is meant is that the wicked tested God and disqualified him as worthy of their attention. It emphasizes the deliberate nature of their rejection.[126] When Romans

---

[123]   *Ibid,* 68.

[124]   *Ibid,* 67.

[125]   G. Berry, *A Dictionary of New Testament Greek Synonyms* (Grand Rapids: Zondervan, 1979), 24.

[126]   Osborne, *Romans,* 55.

1:28 is seen in context of Romans 1:19, 21, what is to be understood is that the wicked have received knowledge of God from creation, tested it and found it unworthy of affecting their conduct.[127] Creation communicates the fact of God to the wicked and the Holy Spirit proves to them their guilt before God (John 16:8-11). Yet they have neglected that voice of God in every instance. This is not passive ignorance but a willful rejection.[128] In addition, the teaching of apostasy says that human beings have a real choice to accept or to reject the Gospel.

Unless we human beings have a *real* choice, we cannot choose life or death (Deuteronomy 30: 19, 20). There is no *whosoever will* (John 3:16); and that God truly desires the death of the wicked. However, Ezekiel 33:10, 11 says: *that He takes no pleasure in the death of the wicked but that they turn from their ways and live.* The desire of God that all would turn is found also in the New Testament. In the New Testament we find the desire of God is that none perish (2 Peter 3:9) but that all would be saved (1Timothy 2:4).

---

[127] *Ibid,* 55.

[128] *Ibid,* 57.

CHAPTER 5

CHOSEN IN CHRIST

In this chapter, the understanding of the doctrine of election will continue as we look at the uses of the word *chosen*. When the word *chosen* is looked at, it will be discovered that not only does election refer to human beings, but election also has reference to Jesus Christ Himself. The Scriptures teach that Jesus Christ has been *chosen* by God (Luke 9: 35). The word used in Luke 9:35, eklegtos, chosen, to describe Jesus is the same word used in Ephesians 1:4 to describe God's choosing of *us*. At this point we will not go into who the *us* refers to. The point here is to state that the same word is used to describe Jesus Christ and us.

Because Jesus is the Chosen One of God; it is important to restate what was stated earlier concerning the person of Jesus. As it was stated earlier Jesus is the Second Adam (1 Corinthians 15:45-47). As the Second Adam, Jesus is an individual who represented the whole (Romans 5:15). In this passage, Paul is contrasting/comparing Adam and Jesus. As Adam represented the whole human race in his sin; so Jesus represents the whole human race in himself and his work of grace. The fact that Jesus is called the Second Adam does point very clearly to the fact that Jesus represents the whole human race. The line of reasoning goes as in this manner. To call Jesus the *Second Adam* means that he must also represent what the First Adam represented. Since the first Adam represented the whole human race; the Second Adam, Jesus must also represent the whole human race.

Jesus, as the representative of the whole human race is seen also in the teaching concerning: For whom did Christ die? The answer to the question of for whom did Christ die is found in the statement that Christ came into the world to save sinners (1 Timothy 1:15). The purpose and mission of Jesus led Him into the world, cosmos, to save sinners. This word, cosmos, is used in the Bible to refer to both the universe[129] and is so used in Acts 17:24 which states that God made the universe and everything in it and cosmos at times is used for the world system and the people in it that has rejected God[130] and is so used in Galatians 6:14. The word cosmos is used to describe either the totality of God's creation, the universe or the totality of the world's system. Thus, when Paul wrote that Christ came into the world to save sinners, the meaning is either or both that Christ came into the universe or the anti-God

---

[129] J. Louw & E. Nida, *Greek-English Lexicon of the New Testament*, 1.

[130] *Ibid*, 508.

system for the purpose of saving sinners. Jesus came to Israel, but His purpose was for the cosmos.

Paul wrote that Jesus came into the world for the purpose of saving sinners. We now ask: who are sinners? The answer to the question: who are sinners is that sinners are the ones who sin. This leads to the question of: who are the ones who sin? Paul writes very explicitly that every single person in the world sins. He states four times in Romans 3:9-12 that every single person sins. Paul then sums up the Biblical position that all have sinned and thus are sinners (Romans 3:23).

Paul states that Christ is the Savior of all men (1 Timothy 4: 9, 10). The Greek *all men* is panton anthropon. Panton, from pas, means the totality of any object, mass, all, every, each.[131] Anthropon from anthropos means male in certain cases but generically means human being.[132] When Paul states that God is the Savior of *everyone*, but especially of believers, he does not mean universalism, or the teaching that everyone will go to heaven. We know this because Paul writes that it is necessary to believe in Jesus Christ to be saved (Romans 10:9-13). What Paul meant when he said that God is the savior of all is that God's grace has appeared to everyone (same Greek words for *everyone* as found in 1 Timothy 4: 9, 10 are in Titus

---

[131]   *Ibid*, 597.
[132]   *Ibid*, 104.

2:11) with the real offer of salvation (Titus 2:11). We know that the offer of salvation is a real offer, that is that Christ died for everyone because it is God's desire, the word for desire is thelo which means *to desire to have, to want,*[133] that all be saved (1 Timothy 2:4). It is also God's desire that none perish (2 Peter 3:9). The word, *perish,* which is used in 2 Peter 3:9 is also used in John 3:16 to describe what will not happen to those who believe in Jesus Christ. Because God desires all to believe and not perish, He sent His only Son to die for everyone's sin (1Timothy 2: 6). In 1Timothy 2:6 it says that Jesus gave himself as a ransom (NIV) for all. The *all* is made clear in 1 John 2:2. In 1 John 2:2 the death of Christ for everyone's sin is made abundantly clear. In this verse, we are told that Jesus is the atoning sacrifice, hilasmos, for the sins of the whole world. Hilasmos means the means of forgiveness.[134] It is explicitly stated that Christ is the means of forgiveness for the whole, holos, which means a totality as a complete unit, whole, entire,[135] world. The death of Jesus for the sins of the whole world is stated by John the Baptist when he said that Jesus is the Lamb of God who takes away the sin of the world (John 1:29). In 1 John 2:2 and John 1:29 *world*

---

[133] *Ibid,* 288.

[134] *Ibid,* 505.

[135] *Ibid,* 597.

is from the Greek cosmos. Thus, the *all* of 1Timothy 2:6 is the whole, entire world; everyone.

The understanding that Jesus died for everyone is taught by Paul in 2 Corinthians 5:11-21. Paul, in this passage teaches that Christ died for all (2 Corinthians 5:14). In this passage the Greek word translated *for* means *for, on behalf of, for the sake of.*[136] The word *all* is from pas, which means *the totality of any object, mass or collective, all, every, each.*[137]The *all* that this passage refers to is all humanity. This is seen in 2 Corinthians 5:15 which states that the *all* from whom Christ died is divided into two categories. The first category is called *those who live.* The second category, by implication, is made up of those who do not live. Paul makes clear the teaching that Christ died for all in 2 Corinthians 5:18-21. In these verses Paul states that God has reconciled the *world*[138] to Himself through Christ (v. 18, 19). This statement agrees with Paul's previous statement that Christ died for all. Paul goes further and states that he was Christ's ambassador and as Christ's ambassador he was imploring people, that is those to whom God is now reconciled, to be reconciled to God (2 Corinthians 5:20). Paul makes

---

[136] *Ibid,* 802.

[137] *Ibid,* 597.

[138] World is from kosmos which means the universe and everything in it (Louw & Nida, *Greek-English Lexicon,* 1.

clear in this passage the teaching that although Christ died for all, not all will accept Christ and be saved when he writes that Christ died for all that we *might* become the righteousness of God (2 Corinthians 5:21). In this verse, *we might* become is in the subjunctive. The subjunctive is the mood of that which is conceivable.[139] This means that Paul wrote that it was conceivable that all might become the righteousness of God, but it was not a certainty that all would be. In 2 Corinthians 5:11-21 we see that God has become reconciled to humanity; it is up to individuals, however, to be reconciled to God. Here again are the same two categories that Paul mentioned earlier in this passage.

What the Bible teaches then is that Jesus died as the means of forgiveness for everyone. The truth is while the offer of salvation is real and Christ truly died for the sins of everyone, not everyone will accept the offer of salvation and be saved (Revelation 2:21). The fact that not everyone will accept the Gospel does not mean that Jesus did not die for them nor does it mean that the offer of salvation is not genuine. Salvation is not automatic. Every individual must repent of his or her sin and accept for him or herself the grace of God in Christ Jesus. It is only then, that the death of Christ for that individual becomes reality for him or her.

---

[139] H. Dana & J. Mantey, *A Manual Grammar of Greek New Testament,* 170.

To understand the meaning of the doctrine of election, it was important to restate what was written in chapter 1 concerning the person of Jesus and His ministry while on the earth.

We now return to Ephesians 1:4 where it says that election is *in Christ*. Since election is *in Christ*; election is connected to both the Person and Work of Jesus Christ. Election in Christ means that no one is elect apart from or outside of Jesus Christ. Neither is election in some decree dis-associated from Jesus Christ. Election *in Christ* also means that the scope of election is intimately connected to Christ's sacrificial death. Shank says that the atonement is both a reflection of the decree of election and the very electing act of God.[140]

Since election is *in* Christ and election is intimately connected to the atonement, the sacrificial death of Jesus, the scope of the death of Christ, that is for whom did Christ die[141] is also the scope of election. Jesus the Lamb of God takes away the sin of the world (John 1:29). Jesus gave His life as an atoning sacrifice (NIV) for the whole world (1 John 2:2). Jesus is the ransom, the price paid to free all men, which means everyone, from sin (1Timothy 2:6).

---

[140]   Robert Shank, *Elect in The Son* (Springfield: Westcott Publishers, 1982), 42.

[141]   Also see above in the discussion of for whom did Christ die.

Since election is *in Christ*, election includes individuals only when they are connected to and part of Christ. This is seen in the words: God chose *us* in Christ (Ephesians 1:4). The *us* consists of believers. Believers make up Christ's Body, the Church. By the use of the word *us,* Paul states that election is corporate and only secondarily individualistic.[142] Shank further posits that the corporate nature of election refers to the Body of Christ and the corporate nature of election includes individuals only when those individuals are connected to the elect Body.[143] This understanding of the corporate nature of election and the inclusion of individuals only when they are related to the Body is accurate only when it is clearly understood that *the Body* refers not to the organization called the Church but to the People of God who make up the true Church. The Body, the People of God are the People of God, only when they are rightly related to and connected to Christ. What this means is that individuals are elect only when they are rightly related to Jesus Christ. This corporate understanding of the nature of election and the inclusion of individuals is strengthened when it is seen that Jesus is also the Chosen One of God (Luke 9:35). As the Chosen One of God it is conceivable to state that all those *in Christ* are also chosen by God.

---

[142] Shank, *Elect in the Son,* 45.

[143] *Ibid,* 48.

A further strengthening of the corporate nature of election and the inclusion of individuals only when those individuals are rightly related to Jesus Christ is seen in the Scriptural teaching on the possibility of apostasy.

The corporate nature of election and the inclusion of individuals only when they are rightly related to Christ is also seen in purpose of election. The purpose of election is to salvation (Ephesians 1:5-7) and to holiness (Ephesians 1:4). All those who are elect are holy; all those who are not holy are not elect. While it is true that all in Christ are holy, holiness as the purpose of election does not refer simply to positional holiness but also to experiential holiness (1 Thessalonians 4:7; 1 Peter 1: 14-16). Because the command of God is that His people live holy lives, there is no certainty of election for those who claim positional holiness and live unclean lives.

There is a question that arises from the understanding of election as primarily corporate. Since election is *in Christ* and Jesus is the Second Adam, does this mean that all humanity is included within the scope of election?

To understand election and the human race; we begin with stating the desire of God for humanity. The Scriptures clearly teach that God takes no delight in the death of the wicked but that the wicked turn from wicked ways and live (Ezekiel 18: 23; 33:11; 2 Peter 3:9). The desire of God is that all would come to salvation (1Timothy 2:4).

Because God desires all to be saved, God provided Jesus Christ, a ransom for all (1 Timothy 2:6) and an atoning sacrifice for the sins of the world (1 John 2:2). What we see from these verses is that God both desires and has provided a means of salvation for the whole world.

The sad reality is that the whole world will not be saved. The world contains within it two groups of people. One group will have eternal life and the second group will be those who endure eternal punishment (Matthew 25:46). This sad fact does not mean, however, that it is God's desire and purpose for those who suffer eternal punishment to do so. The fact that not all will be saved does not mean that God has chosen some for eternal life and the remaining to eternal damnation. God has the same compassion for every individual in the world. The compassion of God is experienced in the truth that God is good to all that He has made (Psalm 145:9). Since God has compassion on all, He did not bring certain individuals into the world in order to punish them.[144]

God has provided Jesus who is both the means of salvation and salvation itself for all. In the death of Jesus was the death of all (2 Corinthians 5:14) and in Christ, God was reconciling the world to Himself (2 Corinthians

---

[144] This was the opinion of many in the ancient world as seen in Josephus, *Antiquities of the Jews*, Book I, Chapter 3, Section 8.

5: 19). Yet, the all as seen in individuals within the human race must choose for him or herself salvation (2 Corinthians 5:15); each individual must choose to accept the fact that God is now reconciled to him or her and thus be reconciled to God (2 Corinthians 5:20).

God's desire is that all would be saved and in that desire provides both the means of salvation and allows individuals the room to choose that salvation. This is seen in the words of Jesus when He said concerning the children of Jerusalem that He wanted to gather them together as a mother hen would gather her chicks, but you, Jerusalem, were not willing (Matthew 23:37). Jesus desired one matter; Jerusalem desired another.

God invites/calls many to enter and to be a part of His kingdom (Matthew 22:1-14). To enter the kingdom is to enter the realm of God, which is by faith in Christ. Thus, when God invites/calls, this call is to life and salvation.[145] The call of God is also to be understood as a call to leave darkness, to enter God's wonderful light (1 Peter 2:9) and to belong to Jesus (Romans 1: 6). The call of God is intimately connected to the atonement, the death of Jesus, since those who are called are those for whom Christ died (Hebrews 9:15). In other words, the recipients of the call of God are the same ones for whom Christ died. The calling

---

[145]   Cranfield, *The International Critical Commentary of Romans, Vol. 1*, 51.

of God is through the Gospel, the message of the death and resurrection of Jesus (2 Thessalonians 2:13, 14) and not through an eternal decree from ages past.

The call of God to life and salvation is not limited to a few. *The many* is used to mean the whole human race[146] as in seen in comparing Paul's use of *all men, everyone* were condemned in the one act of disobedience (Romans 5: 18) and *the many* were made sinners through the same one act of disobedience (Romans 5:19). The call of God is meant for all those in whom God has given breathe and who walk upon the earth (Isaiah 42:1-6).

God calls all to Himself. This is seen in Romans 9:25, 26 where the words *to call* are used twice to describe the acceptance of those who formerly were not accepted. See also 1 Peter 2:9, 10 where those who are called out of darkness, were once not a people, but are now the people of God. Thus, it is to be understood that the call of God is a universal call.

There are those who will object to the understanding of *call* being a universal call. This objection is stated in this manner: No one comes to Jesus unless the Father draws that one (John 6:44). Jesus, in John 6:44 does not limit those who are drawn by the Father. Jesus later on in the Gospel of John gives the scope of the call of God when He said that when He is lifted up, He will draw

---

[146] *Ibid,* 285.

all to Himself (John 12:32). This passage, if taken out of context, maybe used to limit the call of God. However, when this passage is placed within the total context of the words of Jesus, there is agreement with the call of God being a universal call.

A further clarification on the call of God is mentioned at this time. God draws not by force; but by loving-kindness (Jeremiah 31:3); which is the Gospel. This means of course, that the Gospel must be preached in word and deed (James 2:17) to all. God has chosen to use the Gospel lived and preached by His people as the method of drawing the world to Himself. The word *draw* has the sense in its meaning of drawn to a certain point.[147] At that certain point, the ones drawn must then make a decision for themselves.

The call of God is not a call that once has been offered and accepted that cannot be rejected. It is possible to accept the call of God to salvation and then to desert, to forsake that call (Galatians 1:6).

Many are called, invited to salvation, few are *chosen* (Matthew 22:14). The word *chosen* refers to belonging to God. Israel was *chosen* (Deuteronomy 7:6); but not all Israel (Romans 9:6), only those who are the children of Abraham (Romans 9:8); that is those who belong to Abraham's line of faith (Romans 9:8). Jesus is the *Chosen*

---

[147]   Trench, *Synonyms of The New Testament*, 73.

One (Luke 9:35). The True Church of God is *chosen* (1 Peter 2:9).

The many, that is all, the whole human race has been invited/called by God to enter salvation and life; few however, accept that invitation, believe and enter the realm of God's kingdom; belonging to God. This understanding is seen both from the words *called* and *chosen*; but also from the context of Matthew 22:14. The context of Matthew 22:14 is a parable concerning the kingdom of God (Matthew 22:1, 2). In this parable, the king sent his servants to those who had been invited (the same word used in Matthew 22:14 translated invited/called) to the banquet to inform them that it was now time to come (Matthew 22: 3). But, those who had been invited/called refused to come to the banquet (Matthew 22:3). The refusal of the ones who had been invited to obey the king's summons (Matthew 22:3-8) expresses very clearly that the call of God can be rejected. God's call is not a fixed decree; but there is room within the call of God for human response.

When the invited/called refused to obey the king's summon; the King finally told his servants to go out and invite/call *anyone* that they found (Matthew 22:9). The invitation was to both the good and evil (Matthew 22:10). The word *good*, agathos, is used to describe positive moral qualities.[148] This word is used in the description of the law as good (Romans 7:12). It is also used to describe the *good* works that are the result of abounding grace (2 Corinthians 9:8). The word *evil* refers to being morally corrupt and wicked.[149] This word *evil* describes those who are not content to be evil themselves, but describes those who are actively involved in the corruption of others.[150] Both the good and the evil were invited to the wedding feast and were already in the king's hall (Matthew 22:10). Many are called; this includes both the good and the evil.

When the king entered the hall, he noticed amongst the crowd who attended the banquet that there was one who was not wearing wedding clothes (Matthew 22:11). The king approached the man without wedding clothes and asked how he got into the hall (Matthew 22:12). The man was speechless before the king (Matthew 22:13). The king then ordered that the man thrown out of the banquet (Matthew 22:13).

The man was thrown out for not wearing wedding clothes. The meaning of wedding clothes is to be understood in the fact that this is a parable concerning the kingdom of God (Matthew 22:1). Because this is a

---

[148]   Louw & Nida, *Greek-English Lexicon of the New Testament,* 743.

[149]   *Ibid,* 754.

[150]   Trench, *Synonyms of the New Testament,* 316.

description of the kingdom of God; the wedding clothes are symbolic of the right type of life that is necessary to enter God's kingdom. Secondly the significance of clothes is found in the Scriptural use of clothing. Clothes in the Scriptures are used to describe a person's relationship with God. White robes are worn by those who have overcome (Revelation 3:5). They are the attire of those whose life is characterized by deeds that are acceptable to God (Revelation 19:8). White robes are worn by those who are Christ's (Revelation 19:14). Conversely, a life that is not acceptable to God; not righteous is described as filthy rags (Isaiah 64:6).

The man was thrown out of the wedding hall because his *clothes,* his life which is to say his heart, were not acceptable to the king. The man was not thrown out of the wedding hall because he was not invited/called; for he was called/invited (Matthew 22:10). However, after receiving the call/invitation, this man did not respond in a manner that resulted in righteousness. He had the opportunity; yet, he chose not to respond to the call of God in a faithful obedient manner.

The man thrown out of the wedding hall was not thrown out because he was not called. In fact just the opposite is true. The man was called. This is an important point to understand. The man was called; the king wanted him to be there. Yet, the king had him thrown out. The man was thrown out because he was dressed inappropriately. The man was rejected not because he was not called; but because he was not clothed in the righteousness of Christ. A person is clothed in the righteousness of Christ only by faith (Galatians 3:26, 27). The man was thrown out of the king's hall, although he was called, because he was not clothed in Christ's righteousness.

Many are called. One should say because of the meaning of *many* that all are called. However, the call of God, the desire of God as seen in the king wanting all to come into his hall for the wedding, does not guarantee the acceptance of the king, of God. God's acceptance is based on a life that is lived to please Him (2 Corinthians 5:9). Many/all are called, not all are accepted into the king's presence and dwelling place. The parable of the wedding garments teaches that there is no guarantee that all those who are called are justified. Many of the ones who are called are never justified. Also, we learn from the parable of the wedding garment that the teaching of the possibility of apostasy, of falling from grace (Romans 11:22) leads us to the conclusion that nowhere in Scripture is it stated that the exact number of those who called and justified will be glorified.

Many are called few are chosen. Many hear the Gospel; few believe.[151] Many are there who have heard the

---

[151]   Wesley, on Matthew 22:14, *Notes on the New Testament.*

call, yet that call no longer shapes or fashions them into new persons. When the call of God no longer is changing a life, the call of God has vanished without a trace.[152] This same principle is seen in the fact that God has reconciled the world to Himself and is now pleading that individuals respond by faith and accept the reconciliation for themselves (2 Corinthians 5:11-21).

Many are called; few are chosen. God makes a decision, humans respond, God can then change his decision (Jeremiah 18: 7-10). Destiny is not fixed. This teaching is seen in the *ifs* of Jeremiah 18:7-10 where the *if* of God is dependent upon people's *if. If* God intends to destroy a nation or kingdom and *if* that nation or kingdom repents, then God will relent and not inflict on that nation or kingdom the disaster that He planned (Jeremiah 18: 7, 8). *If* God announces that a kingdom or nation is to be built up and planted, and *if* that kingdom or nation does evil in God's sight and does not obey God, then God will reconsider the good that He had intended to do to that kingdom or nation (Jeremiah 18: 7-10).

The teaching that God will reconsider His intentions is taught also in Hosea 11:8. Hosea 11:8 not only teaches that God's intentions can change when people either

---

[152] Eduard Scheweizer, translated by David Green, *The Good News According to Matthew* (Atlanta: John Knox Press, 1975), 421.

repent or reject Him; but this passage also teaches that the heart of God can be changed. The word *changed* (NIV) is hapak. Hapak has the meaning of a change in attitude.[153] When the fact that God's heart can be changed and that there is room in the intentions/decrees of God for human response; this tells us that God's foreknowledge is not causative.

God knows all things, even before the events occur. However, the fact that God's heart can be changed which also means that God's foreknowledge is not causative leads us to the understanding that election, though according to God's foreknowledge (1 Peter 1:2) is not to be understood as limiting God's love and grace to a certain few. In addition, since election is according to the foreknowledge of God; election is not based on some decree in eternity past that separates humanity into two groups: one group the recipient of God's grace and the other group being denied God's grace.

When God calls it is to His purpose (Romans 8:28); which is moral conformity to His Son (Romans 9:29). Christians are exhorted to make certain their calling and election (2 Peter 1:10) which is by cultivating and growing the qualities found in 2 Peter 1: 5-7. Jesus said that it is by their fruit that you and they themselves will know that

---

[153]   Harris, *Theological Wordbook of the Old Testament, Vol. 1*, 222.

they are called (Matthew 7:20). The call of God must be incorporated with the teaching that God will reconsider His intentions based on human response. When it is seen that the call of God and God reconsidering His intentions based on human response are incorporated, this leads to the understanding that predestination is of the means of salvation (Romans 9:8, 12) and not a fixing of the destiny of individuals.

CHAPTER 6

FREE WILL AND FREE GRACE

The previous chapter described the all of God as a universal call. There are those who will object to the understanding of *call* being a universal call. This objection is stated in this manner: No one comes to Jesus unless the Father draws that one (John 6:44). The understanding of this objection is that not all are drawn by the Father. A further principle that underlies this objection is that if all were drawn by the Father, all would come. However, this objection has been addressed throughout this chapter and will be again in this chapter.

We begin with the understanding that Jesus, in John 6:44 does not limit those who are drawn by the Father. Nowhere in John 6:44 is there a limit set on those who are drawn. Jesus simply says that no one comes to Jesus unless that person is drawn by the Father. Jesus is stating a universal principle. This principle is that within a vacuum, if one ever existed, no one would come to belief in Jesus. A further understanding of the words of Jesus in John 6:44 is that the Father is involved in the work of redemption.

The Father draws people to Jesus. The word *draw* has the understanding, not of by force or against the will, but divine attractions of love.[154] This is further stated in Jeremiah 31:3 where it states that God draws with loving-kindness. The Father draws people to Jesus by loving-kindness not by some irresistible grace.

The idea of love and not grace that is irresistible that draws people to Jesus is seen in the word nadab. Nadab means an uncompelled and free movement of the will to divine service or sacrifice.[155] Nadab is used in Exodus 25:2 where each man is to bring an offering to God that has its origin within a heart that prompts (nadab) him to give. Nadab is used in Leviticus 7:16 and Psalm 54:6 to describe a *freewill* offering. Nadab is used in Hosea 14:4 to describe the love of God as that which is something that is unforced; something that is freely given. In the discussion regarding nadab, Girdlestone has several revealing factors. The first factor is that Girdlestone in his book *Synonyms of the Old Testament* includes his discussion of nadab under the heading of *Freedom of the Will*.[156] The second factor is his discussion of nadab itself. He says in discussing nadab, that nadab means voluntary action as opposed to that which is constrained or compulsory.[157] The Father draws people to Jesus, not by an irresistible grace, but by a love that is freely given.

---

[154]   Trench, *Synonyms of the New Testament,* 72.

[155]   Harris, *Theological Wordbook of the Old Testament*, 554.

[156]   Girdlestone, *Synonyms of the Old Testament,* 70.

[157]   *Ibid,* 70.

This idea of love that can be resisted as that which draws people to Jesus is seen in Matthew 23:37. In this passage Jesus said that He longed to gather Jerusalem together as a mother hen gathers her chicks, but Jerusalem was not *willing*. There is in this passage the longing of Jesus' heart, as seen in the word thelo. Thelo means purpose based upon a desire, a preference, a longing.[158] Berry adds that thelo is the will urging on to action.[159] The understanding, then of thelo is that thelo is more than a wish; it is something that lies within the heart and urges on to action, to completion. Jesus further states that people would have life if they came to Him; yet, they will not come to Him, because they do not desire Him (John 5:40). There is life for all who will come to Jesus, yet, so many will not come to Him, not because they are bound by some eternal decree of God, but because they simply do not want Jesus. Choose life or death, God says. He then leaves people with wills enlightened by the True Light, one can also say with grace saturated wills, to their own choice.

In addition to the desire of Jesus, human response is also included in Matthew 23:37. Jesus longed to gather the children of Jerusalem to Himself, but they were not

---

[158] Louw & Nida, *Greek-English Lexicon,* 357.

[159] George Berry, *A Dictionary of New Testament Greek Synonyms* (Grand Rapids: Zondervan, 1979), 25.

willing. The unwillingness of Jerusalem to be gathered to Jesus is thelo, the same word used to describe the heart longing of Jesus is used to describe the unwillingness of Jerusalem to come to Jesus. Jesus longed for one thing; Jerusalem longed for another. The heart of Jesus longed for one matter; the heart of the people of Jerusalem longed with the same intensity another matter.

Jesus later on in the Gospel of John gives the scope of the call of God when He said that when He is lifted up, He will draw all to Himself (John 12:32). In John 6:44 the truth is stated that the Father is involved in the work of redemption in that He is involved in the drawing of people to Jesus. The truth is that no one comes to Jesus unless that person is drawn, attracted. Because the scope of the attraction is the world and many in the world do not come to faith in Jesus; it can be seen that this attraction, this grace is not irresistible.

God's grace, the longing, the drawing of both the Father and of Jesus of the human race which is not irresistible, which means people can reject the grace, the drawing of God; leads to the discussion of the *freedom of the will*. If God's grace is not irresistible, is the human will free?

The Bible states that there are willing hearts (2 Chronicles 29:31; Exodus 25:2; 35: 21, 22; 35:5); a willing spirit (1 Chronicles 28:9; 29:5; Psalm 51:1, 2; 1 Corinthians

9:17; 1 Peter 5:2); a willingness to give to God (Exodus 25:2; 35:29; Judges 5:2, 9; 1 Chronicles 29:9, 17); freewill offerings (Leviticus 22:18, 21, 23; 23:38; Numbers 15:3; 29:39; Deuteronomy 12:6, 17; 16:10; 23:23; 2 Chronicles 31:14; Ezra 1:4; 3:5; 7:13, 16, 8:28; Psalm 119:108); a spirit that is spontaneous and not forced (Philemon 14).

When the many passages that refer to freewill offerings is examined; what is discovered is that the word translated *freewill offering* is from nadab.

However, to return to the question: is the human will free? We must understand the context in which this question is framed within the theological discussion in which is found. The meaning of *free will* in theological discussions centers around the idea of the human will being free both from the effects of sin and able to respond, on its own, to God apart from God's grace. When the idea of *free will* is understood within this context, then the clear answer is no, the human will is not free. The human will has been affected by sin. In addition, the human will apart from God's grace cannot respond to God.

There is no human will that is free in the sense of being unaffected by sin nor free from God's grace. God sends His Spirit to aid the human individual in the choice that is to be made. This is seen in the description of Jesus as the true light (John 1: 9). As the true light, Jesus gives light to every man (John 1:9). The phrase *every man* is from the Greek *pas anthropos*. Pas means the totality of any objective, mass, collective.[160] Anthropos means human being.[161] Thus, *pas anthropos* means the totality of the human race. In addition, since every man is singular rather than plural; the singular every man is meant to indicate every man individually rather than all men in mass.[162]

Jesus, the light of the world, enlightens every person. While it is true that those who do not believe are yet in darkness (John 3:19); yet, there is a general illumination of the human race.[163] The general illumination of the human race is found in the words of Paul who wrote that God has revealed something of Himself to all men and this revelation is sufficient for them to be blameworthy, without excuse (Romans 1:20). This general illumination is the activity of the Word.[164]

Jesus, the light of the world (John 8:12) is also the life of men (John 1:4). In this verse, men is the plural of anthropos, which would mean mankind, humanity, in

---

[160] Louw & Nida, *Greek-English Lexicon of the New Testament,* 597.

[161] *Ibid,* 104.

[162] Leon Morris, *The Gospel according to John* (Grand Rapids: Eerdmans, 1971), 9.

[163] *Ibid,* 95.

[164] *Ibid,* 95.

mass.[165] Morris says that because there is life in the logos, there is life in everything on the earth. Life does not exist in its own right.[166]

As the light and life of man individually and of the race collectively, Jesus is shining continually. This is seen in the present tense of the verb *shining* in John 1:9. Even if unbelievers are still in darkness, the light of Christ still shines on them.[167] This is seen in the fact that when Jesus walked this earth, there were many who did not believe, yet the light of Christ's presence shone on them. It was impossible for anyone to be in the presence of Jesus and avoid the light that He is. The light of the world is shining on everyone, this is true whether they walk in it or turn their backs against it.[168] The present tense in John 1:9 also states that grace is not something that is given once. Grace is continually given; even if not acted upon.

Jesus, the true light is giving light to every human being. This is done by means of the conscience[169] and by means of the Holy Spirit who convicts the world[170]

---

[165]   Louw & Nida, *Greek-English Lexicon,* 104.

[166]   Morris, *The Gospel According to John,* 83.

[167]   John Marsch, *Saint John* (Philadelphia: The Westminster Press, 1968), 106.

[168]   Morris, *The Gospel According to John,* 84.

[169]   J. Wesley on John 1:9 in his *Notes on the News Testament* (Kansas City: Beacon Hill Press, 1983).

[170]   World is kosmos which means the entire universe and everything in it (Louw & Nida, *Greek-English Lexicon,* 1).

in regard to sin and righteousness and judgment (John 16:8-11). The conviction of the world by the Holy Spirit in regard to sin is because the whole world does not believe in Jesus (John 16:9). The conviction by the Holy Spirit in regard to righteousness because Jesus is going to the Father; and finally, the conviction in regard to judgment because the Prince of this world now stands condemned (John 16:10, 11).

When is the light given to everyone? The phrase in John 1:9 says that the enlightening of everyone occurs *while coming into the world.* This phrase, while coming into the world, can modify either the true light or man. If the coming into the world modifies every man, then the meaning is at each person's birth they begin to receive the light. If the phrase modifies the true light, which is Jesus, then the meaning is when Christ came into the world, He enlightens everyone. Since John 1:9 is part of a section that discusses the incarnation of Jesus, the meaning would seem to mean that it is when the true light came into the world.

If Jesus enlightened all people when He, Jesus, came into the world, this does not necessarily mean that the light is given to everyone at the birth of Jesus. In the light of the clear statement that Jesus is enlightening all people, the question of those who were born, lived and died before the birth of Jesus would need to be asked. Once they had died, how were they enlightened by Jesus at His birth?

To understand how Jesus is enlightening all people, we begin with the fact that the light has been in existence from the beginning of creation (Genesis 1:3). In addition, the relationship of light and life with God did not begin at the physical birth of Jesus but is an eternal principle found in the person of God (Psalm 36:9). Furthermore, Revelation 13:8 states that the Lamb was slain from the foundation of the world. There are those who connect the phrase, *from the foundation of the world*, to names being written in the Lamb's book of life, since the same phrase is found in Revelation 17:8. However, to state categorically that the phrase in Revelation 13:8 is to be connected to the writing of names in the Lamb's book life based solely on the fact that it is stated in Revelation 17:8, may or may not be the correct step. In Revelation 13:8, the phrase, *from the foundation of the world* follows immediately after the Lamb who was slain. Beasley-Murray states: *it may be safely said that no group of translators would have come to such a decision (tying it to written before foundation of world) were it not for the statement in Revelation 17:8, for the phrase in question immediately follows, the Lamb was slain.*[171] There is also the statement found in the

---

[171] G. R. Beasley-Murray, *The Book of Revelation* (Greenwood: The Attic Press, 1974), 213.

Assumption of Moses 1:14: *Accordingly He designed and devised me, and He prepared me before the foundation of the world, that I should be the mediator of His covenant.* If this statement is to be taken at face-value, then Moses, the first mediator of God's covenant was prepared before the foundation of the world. Could not also Jesus, the second, perhaps better to state the primary mediator between God and humanity (1 Timothy 2:5) have been slain from the foundation of the world? When the slaying of the Lamb of God is connected to before the foundation of the world, the meaning is not that Jesus died before the foundation of the world. Jesus died in history under Pontius Pilate. In fact, this is the Scriptural teaching regarding Jesus, the Lamb of God, who was chosen before the foundation of the world, but was revealed in the last days (1 Peter 1:19, 20).

Jesus, the Lamb of God, chosen before the foundation of the world, yet, was revealed in the last days. There is in this passage the teaching that the need for redemption was understood and incorporated into the plan of God from even before creation. Although God wove into the fabric of creation redemption (see Genesis 3:15, the first proclamation of the Gospel); the actual out-working of this plan occurred in time. There was never a time when the creation was devoid of redemption and its' out-working. Redemption, as found in the person of Jesus Christ has been an integral part of creation since before the foundation of the earth was laid. What connecting the slaying of the Lamb of God to before the foundation of the world would mean is that the principle of sacrifice and redemption is older than the world. It belongs to the essence of the Godhead[172] and that the sacrifice of the Lamb of God lay hidden in the heart of God from all eternity and expresses the very nature of God.[173]

Jesus, the light of the world, is enlightening all people when He came into the world. Based on the teaching that redemption has been a fabric of creation and is part of who God is and on the fact that Jesus, the Lamb of God has also been a part of creation from the beginning, the coming of the Lamb of God, the Second Person of the Trinity, into the world did not happen at the birth of Jesus, but the Lamb of God, the Second Person of the Trinity has always been a part of creation, since He is the one who holds all things together in Himself (Colossians 1:17) and who sustains all things by means of His powerful word (Hebrews 1:3). Yes, it is true that the Incarnation occurred in time. Jesus was born, lived, died, rose and ascended in time; yet, the Son of God is and has been an integral part of creation from the time of creation itself up to present and into the eternity.

---

[172] RH Charles, *A Critical and Exegetical Commentary on the Revelation of St. John* (Edinburgh T&T Clark, 1975), 534.
[173] Beasley-Murray, *The Book of Revelation,* 214.

Since the Son of God, the Second Person of the Trinity is and has been the one who holds all things together, and since Jesus is the light and life of humanity in mass and individuals in particular; it is to be understood that the enlightening of God has been a part of creation as well from before the foundation of the world. When did Jesus begin to enlighten all people? The answer to the previous question is that Jesus began to enlighten all people from before the foundation of the world. The ever present enlightening of the Second Person of the Trinity is the only context that gives meaning to the evidence for God in creation and the conviction of the Holy Spirit by which people are without excuse before God.

We return to the original question of this chapter: Is the human will free? The answer to that is no. The human will is not free from the corruption of sin. Because the human is not free from the corruption of sin, the human will cannot respond to the Gospel, apart from God's grace. While it is true that the human will is not free from sin's corruption; the human will is not bound either. The idea of bound comes again from the theological discussions regarding the will. The bondage of the will states that the will is not capable of choosing God, because it is devoid of grace. The teaching on the enlightening by Jesus of all people reveals that the human will, even after the Fall is not devoid of grace.

To understand the inter-relationship of grace and the human will, it is important to understand that human individuals are not spiritual or non-spiritual in his or her essence. While it is true that every human person fits into one of two categories: spiritual—that is having been born-again or non-spiritual—that is not having been born-again. The reality is that in their essential makeup, all human beings are spiritual. This certainly is not saying that all people are born-again or will go to heaven. The meaning that all persons are spiritual is that there runs through and within the fabric of creation, which includes the human race, the breath, the spirit of God (Genesis 1). There is not one aspect of creation that is totally devoid of God's breath or God's grace. Creation is saturated with God's presence. The saturation of creation with the Spirit of God is seen also in the creation of the human race. When God created Adam, God breathed into Adam's body, the breath of life (Genesis 2:7). A further description of the saturation of creation with the Spirit of God is seen in that it is in Jesus Christ that everything is held together (Colossians 1:17).

It is true that at the Fall humanity rejected and turned from God. When humanity rejected and turned from God, sin corrupted the total person. There is not one aspect of the human individual that has not been corrupted by sin. The Fall, however, while defacing the image of God within humanity, did not strip the image of God from humanity, nor did the Fall cause the breath, the grace of God to depart from the race. Humanity, though fallen and sinful, still retained the image of God (Genesis 9:6; James 3:9).[174]

An aspect of the image of God is God's breath. It is God's breath that gives life to every single person (Genesis 2:7). If God were to withdraw His breath from people, they would die and their bodies return to the dust (Psalm 104:29). The presence of God's breath is life; the absence of God's breath is death. This death includes physical death, since when God withdraws His breath people will die and return to the dust (Psalm 104:29). There does not exist a single human being living in this world who does not have the breath of God within them. Even after the Fall, in the midst of sin, every person still has the breath of God, which is life within them. While the breath of God remains within a person, that person is the recipient of God's presence, God's grace. What is to be understood from this is that even after the Fall, creation and humanity were still saturated with the breath of God.

The human will, as an aspect of the human person, even after the Fall is saturated with the breath of God and is also the recipient of the enlightenment of the True Light.

---

[174] W. Brueggemann, *Genesis* (Atlanta: John Knox Press, 1982), 82.

This enlightening by the True Light has been occurring from the time that the Son of God began the work of creation and the work of holding all things together in Himself. In other words, the human will, not being an entity free apart from God's grace; has always been the recipient of God's grace seen in the enlightening of the True Light and the presence of the breath of God.

The enlightening grace of God is experienced in the conscience. Every person, except a small minority whose conscience is seared beyond all sensitivity, has a conscience which recognizes to some degree right and wrong. The conscience[175] and the heart of individuals and of humanity in mass have been *imprinted* with the essence of the Law; those truths that God both is and those what requires from individuals (Romans 2:15). Paul wrote, concerning the inner meaning of the Law that even on the hearts of the Gentiles these truths have been written (Romans 2:15). There is no one, except that small minority whose conscience is so insensitive to right and wrong, that do not have a conscience which at times accuses them of wrongdoing or defends the person for doing what appears to be right (Romans 2:15).

---

[175] Conscience is the psychological faculty which can distinguish between right and wrong (Louw & Nida, *Greek-English Lexicon of the New Testament*, 324).

The enlightenment of the True Light occurs within and through the conscience. The sense of right and wrong is a part of being created in the image of God and is the recipient of the enlightening grace of God. Every desire to do what is right, and it must be understood that the right is not nor never has been separated from what God considers right, is from God (Philippians 2:13). While it is true that in Philippians 2:13 Paul is talking about working out one's salvation (Philippians 2:12); he makes a more fundamental statement that he echoes in Romans 2:15 that is within the hearts and consciences of people, God's grace operates.

Wesley sums up the teaching of the enlightening grace of God when he says: *Allowing that all the souls of men are dead in sin by nature, this excuses none, seeing there is no man that is in a state of mere nature; there is no man, unless he has quenched the Holy Spirit, that is wholly void of the grace of God. No man living is entirely destitute of what is vulgarly called 'natural conscience'. But this is not natural; it is more properly termed 'preventing grace'*[176]. *Every man has a greater or lesser measure of this, which waiteth not for the call of man. Everyone has sooner or later good desires, although the generality of men stifle them before they can strike deep root or produce any considerable fruit. Everyone*

---

[176] Preventing grace is called *general illumination* by others.

has some measure of that light, some faint glimmering ray, which sooner or later, more or less, enlightens every man that cometh into the world. And everyone, unless he be one of the small number whose conscience is seared as with a hot iron, feels more or less uneasy when he acts contrary to the light of his own conscience. So that no man sins because he has not grace, but because he does not use the grace which he hath.[177]

At this point it is important to understand that Wesley believed in the corruption of the will and of human nature.[178] However, while teaching the total corruption of the human; he held to the Scriptural teaching that the True Light is enlightening (present tense in the Greek) all people. What this means is that in the midst of corruption, God has not left Himself without a witness. The grace of God experienced in and through the conscience has healed to a degree the will. The will of individuals is healed because the breath of God is life (Genesis 2:7). Since the presence of the breath of God is life and the very presence of God's breath, which is also grace-filled, enables the will to respond to the Gospel. We can say that the breath of God heals to a degree the human will and

---

[177] J. Wesley's sermon, *On Working Out Our Own Salvation.*
[178] J. Wesley's sermon, *The Way to the Kingdom.*

thus enables the human will to respond either with a yes or a no to the Gospel.[179]

The human will, being the recipient of the grace of God has been enabled by the enlightening of the True Light to be able to respond to the Gospel. This does not mean, however, that everyone will respond to the Gospel. Individuals who have the ability to respond do not always make the right response. Maddox states that God's grace, while it empowers our response does not coerce it.[180] The ability to respond does not always lead to the right response. God has not only created within His intentions/ decrees room for human response; He has enlightened the human will so that individuals have the ability to respond to the Gospel. Truly, every single human person stands without excuse before the Almighty God for his or her response or lack of.

The fact that the human will is saturated with the grace of God means that human beings have the ability to make decisions. This fact is also seen in the creation of human beings. Humanity was created in the image of God (Genesis 1:27). Even after the Fall, humanity still retained the image of God (Genesis 9:6) and the breath of God is still the life force of every human person (Genesis

---

[179] R. Maddox, *Responsible Grace* (Nashville: Kingswood Press), 1994), 86.

[180] *Ibid,* 86.

2:7). The breath of God will be the life of every person until that person dies, the body returns to the dust and the breath of God returns to God (Psalm 104:29).

Human beings have been created in the image of God. An aspect of being created in God's image is the ability to create. This is seen in the ability to reproduce children after our own image (Genesis 1:28). Another aspect of the God's image is the ability to make decisions that last (Genesis 2:19, 20).

As those created in the image of God with the breath of God as our life force, we have the ability to make decisions that are not forced by God or other outside sources. We have the ability to make decisions that are free. What this means is that we are all responsible for the decisions that we make or do not make. A corollary of this is that God does not cause everything to happen. God does not predestine that someone will be murdered, raped, molested or achieve something positive. If God does predestine that someone is to be raped or murdered, then, since, in this thinking, nothing happens outside of God's will, outside of what God wants to happen, outside of what brings joy to God, then God is the murderer, God is the rapist. Not only does God become the murderer and rapist, but God enjoys it as well. It is also to be seen that if God predestines murder, rape, etc. than the serial killers, serial murderers, serial rapists are the most God-like of all.

A further corollary to be seen is that if God predestines murder, rape, etc. He becomes the monster, the most vile of all beings.

There are some who say that God does cause all things to happen. In support of this, Romans 8:28 is quoted. However, when Romans 8:28 is studied, it will be seen that the meaning is quite different. Romans 8:28 can be understood from the Greek as meaning either: all things work together for good or God works all things together for good. There is not unanimity in agreement amongst either the scholars or the Greek manuscripts. However, that being said, we then proceed to the verb *work together with* (sunergei). This word means to engage in an activity together with someone else, to work together with, to be active together with.[181] Since the meaning of sunergei is to work together with, the question is of who? Who is working together with who? The answer is that God is working together with all things to bring about a certain purpose. This purpose is *good.*

In addition, Romans 8:28 refers to God working together with all things for good *for those who love God.* This passage does not refer to those who do not love God. Thus, this verse does not support the statement that God causes all things.

---

[181]   Louw & Nida, *Greek-English Lexicon,* 512.

Furthermore, Romans 8:28 does not say that God *causes* all things, or that God caused something to happen. What this verse tells us is that when things happen, at least for those who love God, as they are the ones being discussed, God is involved in making good out of the all things, which includes good and bad.

We need to look deeper at the statement that God causes all things. God causes all things means that God not only intends, but brings to reality all things. In addition, God only does what He desires to do since nothing is able to force God to do something that He does not want to do. Furthermore, since God not only does what He wants to do, but is pleased with what He does (Genesis 1:31); God is pleased with all things that He causes. Jesus, the Second Person of the God-head is both the agent of creation (Colossians 1:15, 16) and the one who holds all things together in Himself (Colossians 1:17). This means that Jesus/God is personally involved in creation and maintaining it.

We take the above thinking into the statement that God causes all things to happen. What is then being said is that God not only causes all things to happen, but God wants all things to happen. In addition, not only does God want all things to happen but God is personally involved in all things that happen.

God is building a house it is said and He cannot allow others to build on that house in a way that is not according to God's plan. If one is to use the imagery of God building a house and says that because of this house God causes all things, then what needs to be understood is that the foundation of God's house and the very fabric that runs through the whole of this house is built on murder, rape, death, sin, violation, filth and lies.

God maybe building a house, however, that house is built, in the midst of evil and sin. This house will be a holy house (Ephesians 2:21). Sin, murder, rape, death, etc. are not a part of God's house.

An aspect of the teaching that God causes all things is that what happens to individuals is either the desire of God for that person or is the direct result of someone's sin. The reality, however, is that to say that what happens to an individual is the direct result of his or her sin is somewhat difficult to reconcile with the teaching that God causes all things. If God causes all things, then God caused the sinful activity to happen. If that is the case, how then can humans reap negative from what God caused to happen? In addition, if God causes all things, people are not responsible for what they do. God is the cause, the motivating force, the one who actually performed the sin, albeit through the body of humans. If God is responsible for all things, then humans cannot be judged for what they are not responsible for; for what God has caused to happen for eternity past.

The teaching that God causes all things is seen in the statement that people get what they deserve. In this life, do people get what they deserve? During the course of this life, is God in the business of handing out punishment? The message of grace tells that this is not so. Grace is gift (Ephesians 2:5, 8). The grace of God as seen in the person of Jesus Christ is cosmic. Jesus' death is the atonement sacrifice for the whole world (1 John 2:2) and his death has cleansed the heavens (Hebrews 9:23). Jesus did not die just for individuals but to reconcile all things to God (2 Corinthians 5:19). We do not receive what we deserve; Jesus took upon Himself what we deserve. Jesus, the Lamb of God, takes away the sin of the world (John 1:29). The word *takes away* is airo which means to lift up, to take upon oneself a burden and thus delivering others from the burden.[182] Jesus did not just bear, take way the sins of a few, but the world (John 1:29). Furthermore, Jesus bore on His body our sins (1 Peter 24). The word bore, anaphero, means to offer up someone or something as a sacrifice.[183]

---

[182] Girdlestone says that airo answers to the Hebrew nasa which means to lift up and thus relieving others of the burden, *Synonyms of the Old Testament*, 138. Louw & Nida state that airo means to lift up and carry away, to remove, to take away, *Greek-English Lexicon*, 207.

[183] Louw & Nida, 534.

Anaphero has the sense of the imposing of the debts of one upon another, in order to free the former from payment.[184] Anaphero means that Jesus took the responsibility of the sin of others upon Himself.[185] In addition, we were under the curse for disobedience, yet, Jesus bearing our sin took the curse instead of us (Galatians 3:13). He became our curse that we might be freed from curse (Galatians 3:13).

The teaching that God gives to us what we deserve is refuted by Paul when he wrote that Christians are not destined for wrath (1 Thessalonians 5:9). The Word of God clearly teaches that the wrath of God will be poured out on those who are disobedient (Ephesians 5:6). In Ephesians 5:6 the word disobedient in its general meaning is an unwillingness or refusal to comply with the demands of some authority.[186] When disobedient is used in a specifically Biblical context, it has the understanding of a refusal to believe the Christian message.[187] The meaning, then, of those who are disobedient are those who reject not only the Gospel message, but the Lord Jesus Himself

---

[184] James Moulton and George Milligan, *The Vocabulary of the Greek Testament* (Grand Rapids: Eerdmans, 1982), 39; William Arndt and F. Wilbur Gingrich, *A Greek-English Lexicon of the New Testament and Other Early Christian Literature* (Chicago: The University of Chicago Press, 1979), 63.

[185] Girdlestone, *Synonyms of the Old Testament*, 138.

[186] Louw & Nida, *Greek-English Lexicon,* 468.

[187] *Ibid,* 379.

as the one who has authority over their lives. When a person rejects the Gospel message and the Lord Jesus, this rejection is not necessarily seen in a life of chaos and anarchy. Adam and Eve rejected the authority of the Word of God and in rejecting the Word of God, they also rejected God as having authority over their lives. Because they rejected God, they lost Paradise. Adam and Eve did not begin to live a life of chaos and anarchy after they were kicked out of Eden. It is possible that Adam and Eve lived a more ethical life than is lived by the vast majority of the world's population today, including Christian believers. What Adam and Eve lost was a personal relationship with God. To be disobedient to the Lord Jesus Christ and to the Gospel message is seen not in an unethical life, but in a life that lacks the Spirit of God (Romans 8:9) and thus that person is unknown on a personal level to Christ (Matthew 7:21-23).

The disobedient are found both within the Christian religion and without. Within the Christian religion are those who, while thinking that they are obedient, are in fact disobedient. There are those who do the right things, but without the right motive. Paul says that it is possible to do the right things, yet, without love (1 Corinthians 13). While 1 Corinthians 13 is commonly known as the Love Chapter, this chapter is also a message that clearly states that the Christian act can be performed without Christ.

It is possible to speak in the tongues of men of angels, to speak prophetically, to understand all mysteries, to move mountains, to given all to the poor and to surrender one's body to the flame (suffer a martyr's death) all *without* love. We are told that God is love (1 John 4:16). To do all the Christian activities without love is then to perform them without God.

Those who are disobedient are those who live out of a selfish motive (Romans 2:8). Many within the Christian world live outwardly Christian lives, say the right things, yet, do not tithe, give to the poor, nor visit the widow or the orphan. These also see their view of Christianity as that which perpetuates a certain lifestyle. This lifestyle maybe seen belonging to the Left and it may be seen belonging to the Right. When Christians think, live, act, vote in a way as to preserve their particular lifestyle and not in a manner that shares the love of God to all equally, this is seen as living out of a selfish motive.

The wrath of God is destined for each and every person, whether Jew or Gentile who rejects the Lord Jesus Christ (John 3:36). In fact, whoever rejects the Son of God, God's wrath is said to *remain* on that person. Remain means to continue to exist, to remain.[188] The meaning of this is that the wrath of God is already on those who have rejected Jesus Christ. Those who at this moment in time

---

[188]   Louw & Nida, *Greek-English Lexicon,* 158.

have not accepted Jesus Christ are already living with God's wrath on them. In summary, then, we see that the wrath of God is destined for those who are not in Christ.

The teaching that God gives to Christians what is deserved does not take into account the truth that in Christ people are forgiven. Forgiveness means that sin is no longer remembered (Hebrews 8:12; 10:17) and that the record of the Christian's sins no longer exists (Colossians 2:14). In Colossians 2:14, the Greek word translated as the NIV's written code means record of debts.[189] The word translated in the NIV as canceled means to cause something to cease by obliterating any evidence, wipe away.[190] Because the record of the Christian no longer exists, the Christian stands before God without accusation.

In the act of forgiveness, one's sins are taken away (John 1:29), which means they no longer exist and the record of one's debts, sins, and wickedness is wiped clean so that there is no longer a record that one's sins existed. The result of forgiveness and the wiping clean of the record of one's debts is that the Christian believer stands before God without accusation (Colossians 1:22). There are two main views of without accusation. One view is that the Christian believer will stand before the Judgment Seat of

---

[189] Louw & NIda, *Greek-English Lexicon,* 394.
[190] *Ibid,* 160.

God and their sins will become known and proclaimed.[191] The purpose of the proclaiming of the sins of the Christian is so that the guilt of all will be known to God.[192] After the proclaiming of the Christian believer's sins, then the announcement will be made by God that the Christian believer is forgiven, the punishment paid.

This view teaches that although forgiven, the Christian believer will still stand before God as guilty. As guilty people, this guilt must be at least proclaimed so that the Blood of Christ will then be seen as the ground for forgiveness and the removal of punishment (1 John 4:18). There is in this view a concern that justice will not be served if there is no recounting of the forgiven sins of the Christian.

The view just stated contains a number of areas that are of concern. The first area is that justice is seen apart from the Cross of Christ. This view teaches that although the Blood of Christ forgives and cleanses, there is still a need for justice. Justice in this view is seen as the Christian receiving what is due him or her. This receiving is not punishment for sin, for that has been taken by Christ. Yet, there is still an understanding within this view that justice must be served. Because Christ has

---

[191] E. Brunner, *The Christian Doctrine of the Church, Faith and Consummation*, 418.

[192] *Ibid*, 418.

endured the punishment for the Christian and thus there is no punishment remaining for the Christian; there is in this view, still the re-counting of the sins of the Christian so that all will know how sinful each and every Christian is or was.

This teaching states that the revealing of the Christians' sins is a complete revealing of the depth of our sin. There are a couple of observations that are to be looked at in light of this.

First of all it is to be understood that a Christian is new, a new person. This new person is righteous. The righteousness of the Christian is Christ Himself (1 Corinthians 1:30). When one is united to Christ, one has the whole of Christ and not simply a part of Christ. It is the total person who is declared right with God at the moment of justification.

The whole person is declared right with God and has received the whole Christ, who is righteousness. It is perhaps well understood, but it must be stated that there is no sin in Christ. Since a Christian is a new person, one created in righteousness and if judgment is a revealing of the depth of one's sin, how then can a new person who in Christ's righteousness have sin?

In addition, it is to be understood that the purpose of the death of Jesus Christ as a substitute for the sinner was also to give spiritual life to the sinner who was dead in his or her sin (Ephesians 2:1-5). This spiritual life is the presence of Jesus Christ, who is life (John 14:6) through the Holy Spirit. The question to be asked is: Are Jesus and the Holy Spirit free of sin? The answer of course is yes. Since Jesus and the Holy Spirit are free from sin, the life that they bring to the believing sinner is free from sin.

The Bible teaches that not only are Christian believers given spiritual life but they have also been cleansed from guilt by the sprinkling, the spiritual application of the Blood of Jesus Christ (Hebrews 10:19-22).

The re-counting of sins committed by the Christian believer even if followed by the proclamation of forgiven teaches that the Christian believer at the Day of Judgment will be humiliated so that Christ exalted. It is true that the Day of Judgment will be a day when Jesus Christ is exalted. The question is: Is Christ exalted by the debasing, the humiliation of Christians or is Christ exalted because of His own obedience? Paul, writing to the Philippians has made clear that Christ is exalted above all because, although Christ was God, He humbled Himself and became human. While human, Jesus Christ became obedient even to the point of death. It is because of Christ's incarnation and obedience that God exalted Jesus and gave Him the name that is above every name (Philippians 2:6-11).

While it is true that Christ's exaltation was due, at least in part to sin;[193] Paul states that the exaltation of Jesus Christ by God the Father was due to His incarnation and obedience and not to the humiliation of the Christian believer.

On the other hand, the Bible is clear in teaching that the one who trusts in Jesus Christ will never be put to shame (Romans 9:23; 10:11). The reason for this is that Christ endured the Christian's shame on the Cross (Hebrews 12:2). Jesus not only bore sin on the Cross (1 Peter 2:24); Christ also took the shame upon Himself that was at one time the Christian's.

A Christian is without shame. The understanding of without shame refers both to now and to the future, especially in the Day of Judgment. If it is true, as some hold that the Day of Judgment for the Christian is a day when all the sins of the Christian are listed and afterwards a proclamation is made of forgiven, is there not to be seen, to be experienced in the recounting of one's sins, shame?

How can one stand before not only God but all other Christians and hear one's sins without a tremendous

---

[193] There is a debate amongst Christians of whether the coming of Jesus Christ into the world was only because of the sin of Adam and Eve or if Jesus Christ would have come into the world even if Adam and Eve had never sinned. This, study, however, is not the place to delve into this debate.

amount of shame? The Blood of Christ not only removes the penalty of sin, but also the shame of that same sin. Christ endured the shame on the Cross. For the Christian, there will be no shame, even, or should it be said especially, in the Day of Judgment.

The second view of without accusation is that the Christian believer not only stands before God free from punishment but also free from accusation (Colossians 1:22). The phrase without accusation pertains to one who cannot be accused of anything wrong.[194] G. Berry goes even further when he states without accusation refers to one against whom there is no accusation, implying not acquittal of a charge, but that no charge has been made.[195]

How can there be no accusation made against those who have sinned? The answer is that Christ by His death on the Cross bore not only sin (1 Peter 2:24) and its punishment (1 John 4:18) but also the total curse of the law (Galatians 3:13). The Blood of Christ has so cleansed both heaven and the Christian believer from sin and its effects that there remains nothing left of sin to accuse the Christian believer of.

In addition, because in forgiveness, sin is taken away (John 1:29) and is no longer remembered by God

[194]   J. Louw & E. Nida, *Greek-English Lexicon,* 438.

[195]   G. Berry, *A Dictionary of New Testament Greek Synonyms,* 17.

(Hebrews 10:17), and the record of one's debts has been wiped clean (Colossians 2:14), there no longer remains any accusation (Colossians 1:22), which means that there no longer is any guilt or shame attached to the Christian believer. No accusation means that there is no shame in Christ (Romans 10:11). No shame in Christ, not only now but also at the Day of Judgment. For there to be no shame at the Day of Judgment, there can be no recounting of the sins of the Christian followed by the proclamation of forgiven. The mere mention of one's sins would bring about tremendous shame, even if the mentioning of one's sins was followed by the proclamation of forgiven.

The Blood of Christ has cleansed the heaven from sin and its effects (Hebrews 9:23-26). Sin no longer stains heaven. Along with the removal of sin, guilt is also removed by the Blood of Christ. This is stated clearly by Jesus when He said that He saw Satan fall from heaven (Luke 10:18; Revelation 12: 9-13). The Devil is the accuser of the Christian believer (Revelation 12:10) and not God. Thus, at the Day of Judgment for the Christian, the One who accuses the Christian believer will not be in heaven to accuse the Christian believer of sin, guilt or disobedience.

The teaching that God gives what we deserve does not take into account the truth that Christians are righteous (1 Corinthians 1:30). This study is not the place to enter the debate amongst the scholars whether the righteousness of

Christians is declared by God that is imputed; or is both declared and actual that is imparted. In both positions, imputed and imparted, the Christian is righteous. One has to ask: What does a righteous person deserve? Does a righteous person deserve suffering, tribulation, etc.? If the teaching that God gives what is deserved, then why do the righteous not receive more blessings?

Jesus took what we deserve so that we might receive what we do not deserve. A foundational understanding of God causes all things and people get what they deserve is that God is the one roaming around seeking someone to punish. This is not true. The punishment of sin occurred on the Cross. Jesus bore the curse, the punishment for sin. What this tells us is that God's grace is everywhere present, active and ministering. Grace is gift (Ephesians 2:8). It is totally undeserved. God offers grace to all. God's grace is offered even to unbelievers. Unbelievers are under God's wrath, yet, grace is what God is offering them.

In direct opposition to the teaching that everything that happens is always a direct result of someone's sin is the words of Jesus. Jesus taught that there is not always a direct correlation between what happens to someone and their personal sin (Luke 13:4; John 9:2). While it is true that there are consequences to our actions, we reap what we sow it is said. When we violate God's laws, we will suffer the consequences

(Romans 1:18-32). However, not everything that happens to people is a direct result of their own personal sin.

Job was an example of someone receiving, not what he deserved because Job was upright and blameless before God (Job 1:8). Yet, Job underwent severe suffering. This suffering, in direct opposition to him getting what he deserved, came as a result of Satan's hand (Job 1:12). There was a time when Satan stood before God and Job was the topic of discussion. Satan accused God of protecting Job and thus Job's righteousness was a sham. God in reply said to Satan that all of Job's possessions, his family, reputation, etc. were in Satan's hands (Job 1:12). The only limit set by God was that Satan could not lay a finger on Job himself (Job 1:12). After this, Satan left God's presence and the calamities began to occur to Job and all he had (Job 1:13-19). What is to be remembered is that Job and all he had were in the hands of Satan and. Satan had authority to perform whatever he wanted to in reference to Job and all he had. If Satan wanted to leave Job alone, he could have. Yet, what Satan did was to use the Sabeans (Job 1:15), fire from heaven (Job 1:16), the Chaldeans (Job 1:17), and a mighty wind (Job 1:19) to take the lives of Job's children and his possessions. It was not God who caused these to happen to Job, but Satan.

What is to be seen in the above is that what happens to individual is the result from three sources. The first source is Satan. He is described as a roaring lion seeking someone to devour (1 Peter 5:8). Unless God and Satan are identical or Satan is a mere puppet in the hands of God, it is Satan who is devouring and not God. As a roaring lion, Satan is also called the Prince of this world (John 12:31); the god of this age (2 Corinthians 4:4); and the ruler of the kingdom of the air (Ephesians 2:2). As the Prince of this world, all the kingdoms and nations have been given to him (Luke 4:6). In addition, there is the possibility that Satan has some control over the climate as he used a mighty wind to destroy Job's family. As the god of this age, Satan *rules* the present evil age and is the unseen power behind all unbelief, wickedness, sin and the results thereof. And finally, as the prince of the air, it is to be understood that Satan is not earth-bound but has corrupted even the heavenly places. The second source from which calamities come is others. In Job's situation, it was the Sabeans and the Chaldeans that were the actual ones to destroy Job's families and to take his possession. Again, unless God and sinners are one and the same, then the Sabeans and the Chaldeans were the instruments, the cause of Job's calamities. As instruments that caused Job's calamities, the Sabeans and the Chaldeans were under the authority of Satan, because all of Job's family and possessions were in the hands of Satan. Since the Sabeans and Chaldeans were under the authority of Satan, they were not under the direct authority of God. The third source from which calamities befall individuals is their own choice. People make choices that are in violation of God's laws and they will suffer the consequences of those choices. This was in essence the arguments of the three who came to discuss with Job the reasons for the calamities. Their position was that the calamities were the result of people's choices. However, these three were not privy to the fact that God had given Job's family and possessions into the hands of Satan.

There will be the cry of *God is sovereign.* Yes, God is sovereign. However, that does not mean that everything comes from the hand and heart of God. If by the sovereignty of God is meant that nothing can happen apart from God's causation; God's doing; then the whole nature of right, wrong, good and evil is changed. If this is the case, then the Serpent is correct in what he said in the Garden in reference to God. The Serpent said that God lied to Adam and Eve, that God is with-holding the best from them, that God is not to be trusted, God is not who He portrays Himself to be (Genesis 3: 1-5).

If God does not love everyone as it is said in Scripture (John 3:16); if Christ did not die for everyone (1 John 2:2; 1 Timothy 2: 4-6; John 1:29); if all people are not enlightened by Christ (John 1:9) and thereby their wills are enabled to make true choices to either accept the Gospel or to reject it (John 3:16—if whosoever does not mean whosoever;

Deuteronomy 30:19, 20); then the Serpent is correct. If God is not who He portrays Himself to be.

If by the sovereignty of God is meant that God causes all things then this understanding is a denial of the Biblical statement of human beings having been created in the image of God. The statement that we were created in the image of God is meant that humans have been given abilities similar, though much less than, to God. An aspect of the image of God is the ability to make choices that have real consequences. Adam named the animals and God did not go behind Adam and re-name them. Adam's choice was real and had real and lasting consequences. The choices that we make, having been created in the image of God, are real choices with real and lasting consequences. This is true, unless God Himself is not able to make choices that have real consequences.

The image of God, which is not lost at the Fall, and being able to make real decisions with real and lasting consequences means that God *honors* the decisions, the choices that we humans make. When it is said that God *honors* the decisions is not meant that God approves, likes or is pleased with all the decisions that are made. What is meant is that God allows the choices that we make to have their full consequences, whether good or bad. Here again, this is part of being created in the image of God.

The cry of the sovereignty of God seems also to be an excuse for individuals to not accept personal responsibility for their actions. If God caused such and such, I am not responsible.

The truth is, however, just the opposite. God works with all things but does not cause all things. He is building in the midst of a fallen world a new people; a people that loves with passion and intensity both God and neighbor. [196]Although humanity has rejected God; God has not rejected humanity (John 3:16). God has not abandoned the world nor is God an evil tyrant waiting to pounce, destroy, rape and kill. God is not the one, at the present time, who is causing or willing the suffering of anyone (Ezekiel 18:32). God is the source of good and perfect gifts (James 1:17). He is not only eager to give good to any and all who ask Him, but He gives without finding fault (James 1:5).

When it is stated that everything that happens is the responsibility of God, what is not understood is that Satan also contributes to what is occurring. Satan, like God, gives wisdom and its results (James 3:14-17). The results of Satan's wisdom, his contribution to life, are envy and selfish ambition. Selfish ambition and envy lead to hate, destruction, greed, and death. These are not from God, but

---

[196]   One can debate whether there is love without passion and intensity.

from Satan (James 3:15). To attribute to God the works of Satan is a dangerous thing to do.

The third of the Ten Commandments states that: you shall not take the Name of the Lord your God in vain. The name of God refers to His person; character; His reputation. The Hebrew word translated *vain* is shaw. The meaning of shaw is emptiness and designates anything that is unsubstantial, unreal, worthless, either materially or morally.[197] Harris further states that shaw points to the fact that taking the Lord's name (i.e. his reputation) in vain will cover profanity, swearing falsely in the name of the Lord, but will also include using the Lord's name lightly, unthinkingly or by rote.[198]

Since the Lord's name is his character, person, reputation, to take the Lord's name in vain is also to teach, to imply, that God is something that He isn't. God states that He loves the world (John 3:16). If this statement is not true, then God is not true to His person. However, since God does not change like a shifting shadow (James 1:17), what He says, He is.

God calls all to salvation and life (Isaiah 42:1-6; Romans 9:25, 26; 1 Peter 2:9, 10). God's call to salvation and life is found in the love of God. Since God loves the world (John 3:16); God's call is to the world. This call of

---

[197] Harris, *Theological Wordbook of the Old Testament, Vol. 2,* 908.
[198] *Ibid,* 908.

God is a real call. The call of God being a real call means that every single individual will have life if they come to Jesus. The call of God to life and salvation is for all, unless God's call is an empty call, which would make God a liar.

Humanity stands before God without excuse. There is ample evidence of God's presence in creation. The True Light is enlightening and enabling the will of every single individual so that it is possible for each person to be able to respond to the Gospel. There is not one person who can stand before God and say: I did not believe because you did not want, choose or elect me. God has chosen all to believe. We are all responsible for the choice of life or death that stands before us.